Vegetation Classification List Update for Amistad National Recreation Area

Natural Resource Report NPS/CHDN/NRR—2011/296

James Von Loh

Cogan Technology, Inc.
8140 East Lightening View Drive
Parker, Colorado 80134

Dan Cogan

Cogan Technology, Inc.
21 Valley Road
Galena, Illinois 61036

February 2011

U.S. Department of the Interior
National Park Service
Natural Resource Program Center
Fort Collins, Colorado

The National Park Service, Natural Resource Program Center publishes a range of reports that address natural resource topics of interest and applicability to a broad audience in the National Park Service and others in natural resource management, including scientists, conservation and environmental constituencies, and the public.

The Natural Resource Report Series is used to disseminate high-priority, current natural resource management information with managerial application. The series targets a general, diverse audience, and may contain NPS policy considerations or address sensitive issues of management applicability.

All manuscripts in the series receive the appropriate level of peer review to ensure that the information is scientifically credible, technically accurate, appropriately written for the intended audience, and designed and published in a professional manner.

This report received informal peer review by subject-matter experts who were not directly involved in the collection, analysis, or reporting of the data.

Views, statements, findings, conclusions, recommendations, and data in this report do not necessarily reflect views and policies of the National Park Service, U.S. Department of the Interior. Mention of trade names or commercial products does not constitute endorsement or recommendation for use by the U.S. Government.

This report is available from NPS Chihuahuan Desert Network website (http://science.nature.nps.gov/im/units/chdn/) and the Natural Resource Publications Management website (http://www.nature.nps.gov/publications/NRPM).

Please cite this publication as:

NPS 621/106585, February 2011

Contents

Tables

Appendix

Executive Summary

The National Park Service (NPS)-Chihuahuan Desert Network (CHDN) and Amistad National Recreation Area (AMIS and NRA), with the assistance of the National Vegetation Inventory Program (NVIP) staff, are preparing to conduct vegetation classification plot sampling in support of creating a vegetation map and geodatabase beginning in spring 2011. As part of study plan (NPS-AMIS 2010) preparation, a preliminary list of 23 ecological systems and component vegetation alliances and plant associations was prepared, primarily from botanical field work conducted by Dr. Jackie Poole in 2004 and the NatureServe Explorer Web site (2010), then vetted by the AMIS species list generated primarily by Dr. Richard Worthington (2002) and Dr. Jackie Poole (2004) to inform the field crews, improve planning decisions, and generate cost estimates for project tasks.

The purpose of Task 3.0: Vegetation Classification List Update for AMIS, is to refine and, when appropriate, update the preliminary classification list of vegetation occurring within AMIS to the vegetation alliance and plant association levels of the National Vegetation Classification (NVC) maintained by NatureServe. The sources of new information include the legacy data evaluated under Task 1.0 of this project, and discussions with researchers sampling classification data on-park.

The plant species list provided by (NPS-CHDN) Biological Science Technician Missy Powell numbered 873 species and varieties (NPS-AMIS 2010) and, with more than 15 legacy research projects evaluated under Task 1.0 of this project, formed the basis for selecting and updating potential vegetation alliances and plant associations occurring within AMIS. The entire updated list presented in tabular form by physiognomic types presents 82 vegetation alliances and 102 plant associations that potentially occur in AMIS. In addition, 52 provisional plant communities described by Poole (2004) are included in this classification list to alert field researchers that previously undescribed communities may be present and should be sampled. There are 15 potential forest and woodland alliances comprising 24 potential associations and 8 provisional plant communities; 33 potential shrubland, dwarf-shrubland, and shrub herbaceous alliances comprising 53 potential associations and 32 provisional plant communities; and 34 potential herbaceous and sparse alliances comprising 25 potential associations and 12 provisional plant communities. As deemed appropriate from the NVC and from legacy research, semi-natural vegetation types characterized by nonnative plant species were included in this classification (representing 10 vegetation alliances and 11 plant associations).

This vegetation classification list will be invaluable as a guidance tool for field crews to apply provisional names to vegetation stands sampled in the field with classification plots, prior to formal classification using statistical analyses. By reviewing this classification list, field crews will also be able to determine when they have encountered a previously undescribed vegetation type. A structured alliance/association list also allows field crews to tally classification plot and observation point numbers on a daily or trip basis to reduce unnecessary field sampling and also to ensure distribution of plots to sample diversity NRA-wide, saving the project time and funding while ensuring thorough vegetation type sampling.

Introduction

CHDN and AMIS, with the assistance of the NVIP staff, are preparing to conduct vegetation classification plot sampling in support of creating a vegetation map and geodatabase beginning in spring 2011. Field crews benefit from having a preliminary list of vegetation alliances and plant associations from which to inform landscape observations of vegetation stands, classification plot site selection, plot density, and community type decisions when sampling vegetation types for classification under the NVC. The list provided herein was prepared using legacy data (analyzed in a companion research report, Task 1.0: Legacy Data Evaluation for AMIS), interviews with researchers directly involved in legacy data gathering, the AMIS plant species list (provided as appendix 1), and NatureServe's Explorer Web site (NatureServe 2010).

The NVC, as developed by The Nature Conservancy (TNC) and currently maintained by NatureServe, represents a national system containing eight levels: (1) Formation Class, (2) Formation Subclass, (3) Formation, (4) Division, (5) Macrogroup, (6) Group, (7) Alliance, and (8) Association, with the finest level being the plant association. Alliances are usually aggregations of associations that are physiognomically uniform and share one or more characteristic or diagnostic species. An association is defined as a plant community or type with a consistent species composition, uniform physiognomy, and homogenous habitat conditions (Flahault and Schroter 1910). The plant association or community type is determined by environmental patterns and disturbance processes.

Associations are separated from alliances through the use of total floristic composition and are named by the most dominant and/or indicator species. For the name or title assigned to an association or alliance, a single dominant species may be used (*Prosopis glandulosa* Woodland). If two dominant species occur in the same stratum a dash is used (e.g. *Acacia berlandieri – Leucophyllum frutescens* Shrubland). If two dominant species occur in different strata, then a slash is used to separate them (e.g. *Prosopis glandulosa / Panicum virgatum* Woodland). Parentheses are used when the diagnostic species are not consistent in the association or alliance (i.e., *Bothriochloa ischaemum – (Pappophorum bicolor)* Herbaceous Vegetation).

The purpose of the NVC is to provide a complete, standardized listing and description of all vegetation types that represent the variation in biological diversity at the community level and to identify those communities that require protection (Grossman et al. 1998). The NVC focuses on existing vegetation rather than potential natural vegetation, climax vegetation, or physical habitats. Because it is not restricted to static vegetation types, classification units are useful both for inventory, site description, and as the basis for building dynamic ecological models. The NVC also includes vegetation along the natural-invasive-cultural (semi-natural and modified) continuum, but it emphasizes natural communities as the focus of biodiversity protection.

The project minimum mapping unit (MMU) is 0.5 hectare (1.24 acres) and vegetation stands are sampled using classification plots. Typically, between three to five classification plots are required to adequately describe most plant associations. Small, unique vegetation patches or stands are often termed "park specials" in the NVIP because of their value for overall management, but they are less than the project MMU. Resource management staff at AMIS identified such stands of unique vegetation at the AMIS Study Plan (2010) kick-off meeting.

Background

The following discussion was excerpted in part from the AMIS Study Plan (2010) and users are encouraged to review the plan to place this classification research study in context with the larger project. Uninundated reaches of the Rio Grande and Pecos and Devils rivers support most of the woodland and forest vegetation types. The majority of AMIS vegetation consists of thornscrub shrubland communities and some sparsely vegetated rock outcrops. A broad drawdown zone can occur on the reservoir shoreline that may be unvegetated or may support shrubland or herbaceous vegetation types if the drawdown occurred over several growing seasons.

The Texas Parks and Wildlife Department (TPWD) (2009) describe this reach of the Rio Grande under the Trans-Pecos, Edwards Plateau, and South Texas Brush Country (Rio Grande Basin) Natural Regions and the Level III Ecoregion of the South Texas Plains, Edwards Plateau, and Trans-Pecos. During 2007-2008, the DHS-USBP used the NVC to describe the vegetation of the Rio Grande floodplain and adjacent toeslopes and canyons in the Del Rio sector (USDHS-USBP 2008). Poole (2004) recorded plant species frequency on pre-selected sites to prepare a plant species list for AMIS, and reported 76 different plant communities. Two major vegetation types are described in the AMIS General Management Plan (NPS 2006); Floodplain/Upland Riparian and Scrub Desert and Thornscrub, as follows:

Floodplain/Upland Riparian: consists of seven general categories including Chihuahuan Desert Scrub, Tamaulipan Floodplain, Thornscrub, Savannah, and North American Arid West Emergent Marsh (USDHS-USBP 2008). The Rio Grande, Devils River, and Pecos River have high water tables and dependable year-round flows and where not confined by steep canyon walls support dense stands of vegetation. Nonnative salt cedar or tamarisk (*Tamarix* spp.) and giant reed or carrizo (*Arundo donax*) are being systematically removed from some reaches of the Rio Grande allowing native riparian and wetland plants to reestablish.

Scrub Desert and Thornscrub: this vegetation structure was compiled from 76 plant communities listed in Poole (2004), 10 vegetative structures from Larson (2002), and corresponding types including Chihuahuan Desert Scrub and Tamaulipan Thornscrub vegetation described by USDHS-USBP (2008). Desert scrub is characterized by shrubs and succulents. Grasses are understory or occur in small patches and typically provide insufficient fuels to carry fire. Scrub Desert occurs on toeslopes, hills, and cliffs adjacent to the river floodplains and above the reservoir high-water line.

Project area vegetation distribution is influenced by several factors (ecologic drivers) that include hydrology, elevation, slope, aspect/slope exposure, precipitation patterns, temperature extremes, topographic position, geology, and soils. The environmental drivers have resulted in a unique assemblage of plant species and plant communities. The environmental drivers are discussed in detail and used to prepare bio-physical unit maps in support of field crews in the companion study (Task 2.0: Gradsect and Field Sampling Plan for AMIS).

The Rio Grande annual flows and sediment delivery/removal have been controlled by Amistad Dam and upstream dams and groundwater pumping for many decades resulting in diminished overbank flooding and allowing bank-armoring vegetation including salt-cedar, giant reed or carrizo, Johnson grass (*Sorghum halepense*), buffelgrass (*Cenchrus ciliaris*), and Bermuda grass

(*Cynodon dactylon*) to become established on riverbanks, point bars, and islands. These invasive, nonnative species have become a management concern and the assignment of AMIS resources to monitor populations and attempt focused control and eradication methods has occurred. Nonnative vegetation types are routinely sampled for classification and mapping purposes under the NVIP.

Legacy Data

Legacy data are existing qualitative and quantitative vegetation information collected in support of a variety of AMIS research projects over the years. Please refer to the companion study (Task 1.0: Legacy Data Evaluation for AMIS [2010]) and the AMIS Study Plan (2010) for an in-depth summary of this project task.

Plant species list development for AMIS was critical to this project task, and three principle legacy studies were undertaken to prepare a comprehensive floristic inventory. In the first, TPWD (1995) botanists in the Texas Natural Heritage Program identified 162 vascular plant species within AMIS, then managed by the U.S. Air force on 107 acres. Secondly, Dr. Richard Worthington (2002) submitted a working draft of plant species known to occur in AMIS. The tabular data were divided into families and each taxa was described by scientific name and author, common name, and known location within the NRA. Listed were 618 species of vascular plants (including club mosses, ferns, and fern allies). The third and most complete species list was prepared by Poole (2004) and totaled 829 taxa. Of these, 706 species were collected in and/or represented by herbarium specimens from AMIS and an additional 123 species had a high likelihood of occurring. Forty-nine plant species collected within AMIS are nonnative and an additional 13 nonnative plant species are expected to occur. Previously unknown AMIS plant species determined from this study were added to the species list provided in Appendix 1.

Also described in Poole (2004) are 76 plant communities (woodland, shrubland, herbaceous, and sparse) determined in the field using a visual estimate of species frequency. The dominant species comprising these communities were used in part to develop the potential list of AMIS vegetation alliances and plant associations (Tables 1, 2, and 3).

Results

The results of this research study are presented in Table 1; a list of 82 vegetation alliances and 102 plant associations was prepared to inform field crew classification plot sampling and guide CHDN-AMIS planning decisions in terms of timing and costs. Additionally, 52 plant communities described by Poole (2004) and not currently present in the NVC were included in the provisional list of vegetation alliances and plant communities to ensure that field crews are aware of potentially new types to sample. A field oversight trip by Cogan Technology, Inc. (CTI) ecologists on December 9, 2009, confirmed the presence of several of the upland and riparian/wetland plant communities included on the list. The final project classification list will appear in the final project report and will be based primarily on new plot data likely collected during 2011; it is unlikely that supplemental legacy data will be available. Additionally, an updated species list will be appended to the project final report and will be available in the project geodatabase.

The preliminary vegetation classification list presented herein supports two AMIS Study Plan assumptions relative to field data collection: (1) sufficient vegetation data occurs for this area that a relatively accurate preliminary list of ecological systems, vegetation alliances, and plant associations was created; and (2) new plant associations and possibly vegetation alliances will be classified from the plot database following field sampling for plots and accuracy assessment points. Vegetation alliances and plant associations listed in Tables 1, 2, and 3 and having an element code (A. or CEGL, respectively) have been previously classified and described on the NatureServe Explorer Web site: (www.natureserve.org/explorer/servlet/NatureServe?init=Ecol). The Poole (2004) provisional plant communities not presently recognized in the NVC are designated with CEGL00xxxx.

For the state of Texas, the NVC currently includes 118 environmental systems, 248 vegetation alliances, and 525 plant associations (NatureServe 2010). When vetted with the AMIS species list of more than 800 taxa, the habitats known for the Trans-Pecos Region and acquired from more than 15 legacy studies, and an oversight field trip, this task resulted in identification of 23 ecological systems, 82 vegetation alliances, and 154 plant associations and provisional communities as possibly occurring within AMIS. The AMIS vegetation inventory area consists of approximately 15,000 upland and shallow water acres and an adequate level of sampling determined in the AMIS Study Plan (2010) was estimated to be between 200to350 classification plots; no legacy plots are considered to be potentially useful, instead all new sampling is recommended.

Because vegetation alliances and plant associations can occur across more than one ecological system, that breakdown (featured in the AMIS Study Plan [2010]) is not used in this task to avoid confusion and repetition. Rather, the list of plant communities presented herein is alphabetized and separated by physiognomic or structural types to be easily and efficiently accessed by field crews. Table 1 includes the forest and woodland types that number 15 vegetation alliances and 24 plant associations (plus eight Poole [2004] plant communities); Table 2 includes the shrubland, dwarf-shrubland, and shrub herbaceous types that number 33 vegetation alliances and 53 plant associations (plus 32 Poole [2004] plant communities); and

Table 3 includes the herbaceous and sparse types that number 34 vegetation alliances and 25 plant associations (plus 12 Poole [2004] plant communities).

Two important uses of the AMIS classification list by field crews are readily identified. The first important use includes documenting vegetation classification plot and observation point collection on a daily and field trip basis to avoid wasteful oversampling, but also to guide representative sampling across the project area so each type is represented by its diversity NRA-wide. Rare types may be sa1mpled as little as one time, while common types may receive 10 to 15 classification plots to document regional diversity. The second important use is to apply the correct provisional plant community name sampled on the vegetation classification plot field form or in the electronic data logger.

Table 1. NVC Forest and Woodland Vegetation Alliances and Plant Associations Identified as Potentially Occurring within the AMIS Vegetation Inventory Project Area

NVC Alliance and/or Association	Common Name	Element Code
Acacia farnesiana - Parkinsonia aculeata Temporarily Flooded Forest Alliance	Huisache - Retama Temporarily Flooded Forest Alliance	A.1908
- Acacia farnesiana - Parkinsonia aculeata Temporarily Flooded Forest	- Huisache - Retama Temporarily Flooded Forest	CEGL007755
Acacia farnesiana Woodland Alliance	Huisache Woodland Alliance	A.660
- Acacia farnesiana / Mixed Grasses Wooded Herbaceous Vegetation	- Huisache / Mixed Grasses Wooded Herbaceous Vegetation	CEGL00xxxx
- Acacia farnesiana - (Prosopis glandulosa) Woodland	- Huisache - (Honey Mesquite) Woodland	CEGL002131
- Acacia farnesiana – Prosopis glandulosa / Aloysia gratissima Woodland	- Huisache – Honey Mesquite / Whitebrush Woodland	CEGL00xxxx
Carya illinoinensis – (Celtis laevigata) Temporarily Flooded Forest Alliance	Pecan – (Sugarberry) Temporarily Flooded Forest Alliance	A.282
- Carya illinoinensis - Celtis laevigata Forest	- Pecan - Sugarberry Forest	CEGL002087
- Celtis pallida – Prosopis glandulosa Woodland	- Granjeno – Honey Mesquite Woodland	CEGL00xxxx
Juniperus ashei Woodland Alliance	Ashe's Juniper Woodland Alliance	A.501
Juniperus pinchotii Woodland Alliance	Pinchot's Juniper Woodland Alliance	A.505
- Juniperus pinchotii / Bouteloua curtipendula - Bouteloua hirsuta Woodland	- Pinchot's Juniper / Sideoats Grama - Hairy Grama Woodland	CEGL004940
- Juniperus pinchotii / Bouteloua gracilis Woodland	- Pinchot's Juniper / Blue Grama Woodland	CEGL002122
Pinus cembroides – Quercus gravesii Forest Alliance	Mexican Pinyon Pine – Chisos Red Oak Forest Alliance	A.392
Populus deltoides Temporarily Flooded Forest Alliance	Eastern Cottonwood Temporarily Flooded Forest Alliance	A.290
- Populus deltoides - Celtis laevigata / Sapindus saponaria Woodland	- Eastern Cottonwood - Sugarberry / Wingleaf Soapberry Woodland	CEGL005025
- Populus deltoides / Panicum virgatum – Schizachyrium scoparium Woodland	- Eastern Cottonwood Switchgrass – Little Bluestem Woodland	CEGL001454
- Populus deltoides – (Salix amygdaloides) / Salix (exigua, interior) Woodland	- Eastern Cottonwood – (Peachleaf Willow) / (Coyote, Sandbar Willow) Woodland	CEGL000659
- Populus deltoides - Salix nigra Woodland	- Eastern Cottonwood / Black Willow Woodland	CEGL004919
- Populus deltoides ssp. wislizeni / Schizachyrium scoparium Woodland	- Rio Grande Cottonwood / Little Bluestem Woodland	CEGL005973
- Populus deltoides (ssp. wislizeni, ssp. monilifera) / Salix exigua Woodland	- (Rio Grande Cottonwood, Plains Cottonwood) / Coyote Willow Woodland	CEGL002685
Prosopis glandulosa Temporarily Flooded Woodland Alliance	Honey Mesquite Temporarily Flooded Woodland Alliance	A.637
- Prosopis glandulosa Temporarily Flooded Woodland	- Honey Mesquite Temporarily Flooded Woodland	CEGL004934
Prosopis glandulosa Woodland Alliance	Honey Mesquite Woodland Alliance	A.611
- Prosopis glandulosa Woodland	- Honey Mesquite Woodland	CEGL00xxxx
- Prosopis glandulosa – Acacia farnesiana Woodland	- Honey Mesquite – Huisache Woodland	CEGL00xxxx
- Prosopis glandulosa / Bouteloua curtipendula – Nassela leucotricha Woodland	- Honey Mesquite / Sideoats Grama – Texas Needlegrass Woodland	CEGL002133
- Prosopis glandulosa - Celtis pallida Woodland	- Honey Mesquite - Granjeno Woodland	CEGL00xxxx
- Prosopis glandulosa / Leucophyllum frutescens Woodland	- Honey Mesquite / Cenizo Woodland	CEGL00xxxx
- Prosopis glandulosa var. glandulosa - Acacia greggii - Celtis pallida / Paspalum setaceum - Urochloa ciliatissima Woodland	- Honey Mesquite - Catclaw Acacia - Granjeno / Slender Crowngrass - Fringed Signalgrass Woodland	CEGL007786

Table 1. NVC Forest and Woodland Vegetation Alliances and Plant Associations Identified as Potentially Occurring within the AMIS Vegetation Inventory Project Area

NVC Alliance and/or Association	Common Name	Element Code
- Prosopis glandulosa var. glandulosa - Celtis pallida / Opuntia spp. - Xylothamia palmeri Woodland	- Honey Mesquite - Granjeno / Prickly-pear species - South Texas Ericameria Woodland	CEGL007787
- Prosopis glandulosa var. glandulosa / (Celtis pallida, Phaulothamnus spinescens, Ziziphus obtusifolia var. obtusifolia) Woodland	- Honey Mesquite / (Granjeno, Snake Eyes, Lotebush) Woodland	CEGL002132
- Quercus gravesii -- Pistacia mexicana Woodland	- Chisos Red Oak -- Mexican Pistachio Woodland	CEGL00xxxx
Quercus fusiformis Woodland Alliance	Plateau Oak Woodland Alliance	A.477
- Quercus fusiformis / Hilaria belangeri Woodland	- Plateau Oak / Curly-mesquite Woodland	CEGL002116
- Quercus fusiformis / Schizachyrium scoparium Woodland	- Plateau Oak / Little Bluestem Woodland	CEGL002115
Quercus fusiformis – Celtis laevigata var. reticulata Woodland Alliance	Plateau Oak – Netleaf Hackberry Woodland Alliance	A.663
- Quercus fusiformis - (Celtis laevigata var. reticulata, Ulmus crassifolia) Woodland	- Plateau Oak - (Netleaf Hackberry, Cedar Elm) Woodland	CEGL002153
Salix exigua Seasonally Flooded Woodland Alliance	Coyote Willow Seasonally Flooded Woodland Alliance	A.649
- Salix exigua / Baccharis salicifolia – Baccharis neglecta / Schoenoplectus spp. Woodland	- Coyote Willow / Mule's Fat – Rooseveltweed / Clubrush species Woodland	CEGL004587
Salix gooddingii Temporarily Flooded Woodland Alliance	Goodding's Willow Temporarily Flooded Woodland Alliance	A.640
- Salix gooddingii Woodland	- Goodding's Willow Woodland	CEGL002743
- Salix gooddingii – Fraxinus velutina Temporarily Flooded Woodland	- Goodding's Willow - Velvet Ash Temporarily Flooded Woodland	CEGL003729
Salix nigra Seasonally Flooded Forest Alliance	Black Willow Seasonally Flooded Forest Alliance	A.334
- Salix nigra / (Cephalanthus occidentalis) Forest	- Black Willow / (Common Buttonbush) Forest	CEGL004773
Salix nigra Temporarily Flooded Forest Alliance	Black Willow Temporarily Flooded Forest Alliance	A.297
- Salix nigra – Celtis laevigata var. laevigata / Baccharis neglecta Forest	- Black Willow – Sugarberry / Rooseveltweed Forest	CEGL007754
- Salix nigra Forest	- Black Willow Forest	CEGL002103
Sapindus saponaria Woodland Alliance	Wingleaf Soapberry Woodland Alliance	A.627
- Sapindus saponaria var. drummondii Woodland	- Western Soapberry Woodland	CEGL004535

Table 2. NVC Shrubland, Dwarf-shrubland, and Shrub Herbaceous Vegetation Alliances and Plant Associations Identified as Potentially Occurring within the AMIS Vegetation Inventory Project Area

NVC Alliance and/or Association	Common Name	Element Code
Acacia rigidula – Leucophyllum frutescens – Acacia berlandieri Shrubland Alliance	Chaparro-Prieto – Cenizo – Guajillo Shrubland Alliance	A.1909
- *Acacia berlandieri* Shrubland	Guajillo Shrubland	CEGL00xxxx
- *Acacia berlandieri* South Texas Plains Shrubland	Guajillo South Texas Plains Shrubland	CEGL002181
- *Acacia berlandieri – Acacia rigidula* Shrubland	Guajillo–Chaparro–Prieto Shrubland	CEGL00xxxx
- *Acacia berlandieri - Calliandra conferta - Castela texana - Forestiera angustifolia* Shrubland	Guajillo – Rio Grande Stickpea – Goatbush – Texas Swampprivet Shrubland	CEGL00xxxx
- *Acacia berlandieri - Diospyros texana - Sophora secundiflora* Shrubland	Guajillo – Texas Persimmon – Mescal Bean Shrubland	CEGL00xxxx
- *Acacia berlandieri - Krameria ramosissima* Shrubland	Guajillo – Manystem Ratany Shrubland	CEGL00xxxx
- *Acacia berlandieri - Leucophyllum frutescens* Shrubland	Guajillo – Cenizo Shrubland	CEGL00xxxx
- *Acacia berlandieri - Quercus pungens var. vaseyana - Quercus fusiformis - Porophyllum scoparium - Perityle lindheimeri* Open Cliff Sparse Shrubland	Guajillo – Vasey Sandpaper Oak – Plateau Oak – Trans-Pecos Poreleaf – Lindheimer's Rockdaisy Open Cliff Sparse Shrubland	CEGL00xxxx
Acacia farnesiana Shrubland Alliance	Huisache Shrubland Alliance	A.1029
- *Acacia farnesiana – Baccharis neglecta* Shrubland	Huisache – Rooseveltweed Shrubland	CEGL00xxxx
Acacia greggii Shrubland Alliance	Catclaw Acacia Shrubland Alliance	A.1036
Acacia neovernicosa Shrubland Alliance	Viscid Acacia Shrubland Alliance	A.1037
- *Acacia neovernicosa / Bouteloua hirsuta - Bouteloua gracilis - Bouteloua eriopoda* Shrub Herbaceous Vegetation	Viscid Acacia / Hairy Grama - Blue Grama - Black Grama Shrub Herbaceous Vegetation	CEGL004244
- *Acacia neovernicosa / Muhlenbergia porteri* Shrubland	Viscid Acacia / Bush Muhly Shrubland	CEGL001342
Acacia rigidula - Leucophyllum frutescens - Acacia berlandieri Shrubland Alliance	Chaparro-Prieto - Cenizo - Guajillo Shrubland Alliance	A.1909
- *Acacia rigidula* Shrubland	Chaparro-Prieto Shrubland	CEGL003874
- *Acacia rigidula – Acacia berlandieri* Shrubland	Chaparro-Prieto – Guajillo Shrubland	CEGL00xxxx
- *Acacia rigidula - Leucophyllum frutescens* Shrubland	Chaparro-Prieto – Cenizo Shrubland	CEGL00xxxx
- *Acacia rigidula - Leucophyllum frutescens - Acacia berlandieri* Shrubland	Chaparro-Prieto – Cenizo – Guajillo Shrubland	CEGL007759
- *Acacia rigidula - Leucophyllum frutescens - Hechtia glomerata* Shrubland	Chaparro-Prieto - Cenizo - Guapilla Shrubland	CEGL007760
- *Acacia rigidula - Acacia berlandieri - Jatropha dioica / Selaginella wrightii* Shrubland	Chaparro-Prieto – Guajillo – Leatherstem / Wright's Spikemoss Shrubland	CEGL00xxxx
- *Acacia rigidula - Acacia berlandieri - Leucophyllum frutescens* Shrubland	Chaparro-Prieto – Guajillo – Cenizo Shrubland	CEGL00xxxx
- *Acacia rigidula - Aloysia gratissima* Shrubland	Chaparro-Prieto - Whitebrush Shrubland	CEGL00xxxx
- *Acacia rigidula - Baccharis neglecta* Shrubland	Chaparro-Prieto – Rooseveltweed Shrubland	CEGL00xxxx
- *Acacia rigidula - Calliandra conferta* Shrubland	Chaparro-Prieto – Rio Grande Stickpea Shrubland	CEGL00xxxx
- *Acacia rigidula - Diospyros texana / Bothriochloa ischaemum var. songarica* Shrubland	Chaparro-Prieto – Texas Persimmon / Yellow (King Ranch) Beardgrass Shrubland	CEGL00xxxx
- *Acacia rigidula - Krameria ramosissima* Shrubland	Chaparro-Prieto – Manystem Ratany Shrubland	CEGL00xxxx
Arundinaria gigantea Temporarily Flooded Shrubland Alliance	Giant Cane Temporarily Flooded Shrubland Alliance	A.795
- *Arundinaria gigantea ssp. gigantea* Shrubland	Giant Cane Shrubland	CEGL003836
Atriplex canescens Shrubland Alliance	Fourwing Saltbush Shrubland Alliance	A.869
- *Atriplex canescens / Bouteloua gracilis* Shrubland	Fourwing Saltbush / Blue Grama Shrubland	CEGL001283
Baccharis salicifolia Intermittently Flooded Shrubland Alliance	Mule's-fat Intermittently Flooded Shrubland Alliance	A.933

Table 2. NVC Shrubland, Dwarf-shrubland, and Shrub Herbaceous Vegetation Alliances and Plant Associations Identified as Potentially Occurring within the AMIS Vegetation Inventory Project Area

NVC Alliance and/or Association	Common Name	Element Code
Baccharis salicifolia – Baccharis neglecta Seasonally Flooded Shrubland Alliance	Mule's-fat – Rooseveltweed Seasonally Flooded Shrubland Alliance	A.987
Bouteloua hirsuta – Bouteloua gracilis – Bouteloua eriopoda Shrub Herbaceous Alliance	Hairy Grama – Blue Grama – Black Grama Shrub Herbaceous Alliance	A.1548
Brickellia laciniata Intermittently Flooded Shrubland Alliance	Splitleaf Brickellbush Intermittently Flooded Shrubland Alliance	A.940
- Calliandra conferta – Acacia berlandieri Shrubland	Rio Grande Stickpea - Guajillo Shrubland	CEGL00xxxx
- Calliandra conferta – Krameria ramosissima Shrubland	Rio Grande Stickpea – Manystem Ratany Shrubland	CEGL00xxxx
Juglans microcarpa Temporarily Flooded Shrubland Alliance	Little Walnut Temporarily Flooded Shrubland Alliance	A.945
- Celtis laevigata var. reticulata - Juglans microcarpa / Leptochloa dubia Shrubland	Netleaf Hackberry - Little Walnut / Green Sprangletop Shrubland	CEGL002166
- Celtis pallida – Prosopis glandulosa Shrubland	Granjeno – Honey Mesquite Shrubland	CEGL00xxxx
Cephalanthus occidentalis Semipermanently Flooded Shrubland Alliance	Common Buttonbush Semipermanently Flooded Shrubland Alliance	A.1011
- Cephalanthus occidentalis / Carex spp. - Lemna spp. Southern Shrubland	Common Buttonbush / Sedge species - Duckweed species Southern Shrubland	CEGL002191
Chilopsis linearis Intermittently Flooded Shrubland Alliance	Desert-willow Intermittently Flooded Shrubland Alliance	A.1044
- Chilopsis linearis / Brickellia laciniata Shrubland	Desert-willow / Splitleaf Brickellbush Shrubland	CEGL004933
Dalea formosa – Mimosa borealis Dwarf-shrubland Alliance	Featherplume – Pink Mimosa Dwarf-shrubland Alliance	A.3568
- Dalea formosa - Mimosa borealis Dwarf-shrubland	Featherplume - Pink Mimosa Dwarf-shrubland	CEGL005009
Dasylirion leiophyllum - (Agave lechuguilla, Viguiera stenoloba) Shrubland Alliance	Green Sotol - (Lechuguilla, Skeletonleaf Goldeneye) Shrubland Alliance	A.850
- Dasylirion leiophyllum - Agave lechuguilla / Bouteloua hirsuta - Bouteloua gracilis - Bouteloua eriopoda Shrubland	Green Sotol - Lechuguilla / Hairy Grama - Blue Grama - Black Grama Shrubland	CEGL004245
- Dasylirion leiophyllum - Viguiera stenoloba - Agave lechuguilla / Bouteloua ramosa Shrubland	Green Sotol - Skeletonleaf Goldeneye - Lechuguilla / Chino Grama Shrubland	CEGL004604
Fallugia paradoxa Intermittently Flooded Shrubland Alliance	Apache Plume Intermittently Flooded Shrubland Alliance	A.934
- Fallugia paradoxa Shrubland	Apache Plume Shrubland	CEGL003875
Flourensia cernua Shrubland Alliance	Tarbush Shrubland Alliance	A.861
- Flourensia cernua / Bouteloua curtipendula Shrubland	Tarbush / Sideoats Grama Shrubland	CEGL001336
- Flourensia cernua / Pleuraphis mutica Shrubland	Tarbush / Tobosa Grass Shrubland	CEGL001541
Fouquieria splendens Shrubland Alliance	Ocotillo Shrubland Alliance	A.863
- Fouquieria splendens / Bouteloua curtipendula Shrubland	Ocotillo / Sideoats Grama Shrubland	CEGL001376
- Fouquieria splendens / Bouteloua hirsuta Shrubland	Ocotillo / Hairy Grama Shrubland	CEGL001377
- Fouquieria splendens / Parthenium incanum Shrubland	Ocotillo / Mariola Shrubland	CEGL001378
- Fouquieria splendens Shrubland	Ocotillo Shrubland	CEGL004452
Gutierrezia sarothrae Dwarf-shrubland Alliance	Broom Snakeweed Dwarf-shrubland Alliance	A.2528
- Indigofera lindheimeri – Senna lindheimeri Shrubland	Lindheimer's Indigo – Lindheimer's Senna Shrubland	CEGL00xxxx
Juglans microcarpa Temporarily Flooded Shrubland Alliance	Little Walnut Temporarily Flooded Shrubland Alliance	A.945
- Juglans microcarpa - Brickellia laciniata / Indigofera lindheimeriana Edwards Plateau Shrubland	Little Walnut - Splitleaf Brickellbush / Creek Indigo Edwards Plateau Shrubland	CEGL004932
- Juglans microcarpa / Cladium mariscus ssp. jamaicense Shrubland	Little Walnut / Jamaica Swamp Sawgrass Shrubland	CEGL004593
- Juglans microcarpa Shrubland	Little Walnut Shrubland	CEGL001103
Larrea tridentata Shrubland Alliance	Creosotebush Shrubland Alliance	A.851
- Larrea tridentata - Agave lechuguilla Shrubland	Creosotebush - Lechuguilla Shrubland	CEGL004562

Table 2. NVC Shrubland, Dwarf-shrubland, and Shrub Herbaceous Vegetation Alliances and Plant Associations Identified as Potentially Occurring within the AMIS Vegetation Inventory Project Area

NVC Alliance and/or Association	Common Name	Element Code
- Larrea tridentata / Dasychloa pulchella Shrubland	Creosotebush / Low Woolly Grass Shrubland	CEGL001269
- Larrea tridentata - Euphorbia antisyphilitica Shrubland	Creosotebush - Candelilla Shrubland	CEGL004564
- Larrea tridentata - Flourensia cernua Shrubland	Creosotebush - Tarbush Shrubland	CEGL001270
- Larrea tridentata - Jatropha dioica var. graminea Shrubland	Creosotebush - Leatherstem Shrubland	CEGL004566
- Larrea tridentata / Muhlenbergia porteri Shrubland	Creosotebush / Bush Muhly Shrubland	CEGL001272
- Larrea tridentata - Opuntia schottii Shrubland	Creosotebush - Dog Cholla Shrubland	CEGL004567
- Larrea tridentata - Parthenium incanum Shrubland	Creosotebush - Mariola Shrubland	CEGL001274
- Larrea tridentata - Prosopis glandulosa Shrubland	Creosotebush - Honey Mesquite Shrubland	CEGL001275
- Larrea tridentata / Sparse Understory Shrubland	Creosotebush / Sparse Understory Shrubland	CEGL001276
- Larrea tridentata / Tiquilia canescens Shrubland	Creosotebush / Gray Tiquilia Shrubland	CEGL004569
Acacia rigidula – Leucophyllum frutescens – Acacia berlandieri Shrubland Alliance	Chaparro-Prieto – Cenizo – Guajillo Shrubland Alliance	A.1909
- Leucophyllum frutescens Shrubland	Cenizo Shrubland	CEGL002168
- Leucophyllum frutescens - Acacia berlandieri Shrubland	Cenizo – Guajillo Shrubland	CEGL00xxxx
- Leucophyllum frutescens - Salvia ballotiflora - Lippia graveolens Shrubland	Cenizo - Mejorana – Redbrush Lippia Shrubland	CEGL007789
- Lippia graveolens – Acacia berlandieri Shrubland	Mexican Oregano – Guajillo Shrubland	CEGL00xxxx
- Lippia graveolens – Acacia rigidula Shrubland	Mexican Oregano – Chaparro-Prieto Shrubland	CEGL00xxxx
- Lippia graveolens – Aristida purpurea Shrubland	Mexican Oregano – Purple Three-awn Shrubland	CEGL00xxxx
- Opuntia engelmannii var. lindheimeri – Salvia farinacea Shrubland	Texas Pricklypear – Mealy Cup Sage Shrubland	CEGL00xxxx
- Parkinsonia aculeata / Cynodon dactylon Shrubland	Retama / Bermudagrass Shrubland	CEGL00xxxx
- Parkinsonia texana – Castela texana – Forestiera angustifolia Shrubland	Texas Paloverde - Goatbush – Texas Swampprivet Shrubland	CEGL00xxxx
Pleuraphis mutica Shrub Herbaceous Alliance	Tobosa Grass Shrub Herbaceous Alliance	A.1551
- Porophyllum scoparium Rock Outcrop Sparse Shrubland	Trans-Pecos Poreleaf Rock Outcrop Sparse Shrubland	CEGL00xxxx
- Porophyllum scoparium / Heterotheca fulcrata – Penstemon baccharifolius Rock Outcrop Sparse Shrubland	Trans-Pecos Poreleaf / Rockyscree False Goldenaster – Baccharisleaf Beardtongue Rock Outcrop Sparse Shrubland	CEGL00xxxx
- Porophyllum scoparium – Perityle lindheimeri Open Cliff Sparse Shrubland	Trans-Pecos Poreleaf - Lindheimer's Rockdaisy Open Cliff Sparse Shrubland	CEGL00xxxx
Prosopis glandulosa Shrubland Alliance	Honey Mesquite Shrubland Alliance	A.1031
- Prosopis glandulosa / Atriplex canescens Shrubland	Honey Mesquite / Fourwing Saltbush Shrubland	CEGL001382
- Prosopis glandulosa / Bouteloua curtipendula Shrubland	Honey Mesquite / Sideoats Grama Shrubland	CEGL002194
- Prosopis glandulosa / Bouteloua gracilis Shrubland	Honey Mesquite / Blue Grama Shrubland	CEGL001383
- Prosopis glandulosa / Cynodon dactylon Shrubland	Honey Mesquite / Bermudagrass Shrubland	CEGL00xxxx
- Prosopis glandulosa / Muhlenbergia porteri Shrubland	Honey Mesquite / Bush Muhly Shrubland	CEGL001511
- Prosopis glandulosa / Pleuraphis mutica Shrub Herbaceous Vegetation	Honey Mesquite / Tobosa Grass Shrub Herbaceous Vegetation	CEGL001641
- Prosopis glandulosa - Ziziphus obtusifolia Shrubland	Honey Mesquite - Lotebush Shrubland	CEGL004939
- Prosopis glandulosa var. glandulosa - Opuntia engelmannii var. lindheimeri - Borrichia frutescens Shrubland	Honey Mesquite - Texas Prickly-pear - Bushy Seaside-tansy Shrubland	CEGL007790
- Prosopis glandulosa var. glandulosa - Parkinsonia texana var. macra - (Cordia boissieri, Koeberlinia spinosa) Shrubland	Honey Mesquite - Texas Paloverde - (Anacahuita, Allthorn) Shrubland	CEGL007762
- Prosopis glandulosa var. torreyana Shrubland	Western Honey Mesquite Shrubland	CEGL001381
Quercus mohriana Shrubland Alliance	Mohr Oak Shrubland Alliance	A.782

Table 2. NVC Shrubland, Dwarf-shrubland, and Shrub Herbaceous Vegetation Alliances and Plant Associations Identified as Potentially Occurring within the AMIS Vegetation Inventory Project Area

NVC Alliance and/or Association	Common Name	Element Code
- *Quercus mohriana - Juniperus pinchotii / Bouteloua curtipendula* Shrubland	- Mohr Oak - Pinchot's Juniper / Sideoats Grama Shrubland	CEGL002173
Rhus trilobata Shrubland Alliance	Skunkbush Sumac Shrubland Alliance	A.3569
- *Rhus trilobata / Bouteloua curtipendula - Schizachyrium scoparium* Shrubland	- Skunkbush Sumac / Sideoats Grama - Little Bluestem Shrubland	CEGL005026
Rhus virens var. *choriophylla* Shrubland Alliance	Evergreen Sumac Shrubland Alliance	A.922
Salix (exigua, interior) Temporarily Flooded Shrubland Alliance	(Coyote Willow, Sandbar Willow) Temporarily Flooded Shrubland Alliance	A.947
- *Salix exigua* Temporarily Flooded Shrubland	- Coyote Willow Temporarily Flooded Shrubland	CEGL01197
- *Salix interior / Phragmites australis* Temporarily Flooded Shrubland	- Sandbar Willow / Common Reed Temporarily Flooded Shrubland	CEGL007753
Salix nigra Temporarily Flooded Shrubland Alliance	Black Willow Temporarily Flooded Shrubland Alliance	A.948
- *Salix nigra* Temporarily Flooded Shrubland	- Black Willow Temporarily Flooded Shrubland	CEGL003901
Salvia ballotiflora – Rhus virens – Diospyros texana Shrubland	- Mejorana – Evergreen Sumac – Texas Persimmon Shrubland	CEGL00xxxx
Sophora secundiflora - Diospyros texana Shrubland Alliance	Mescal Bean - Texas Persimmon Shrubland Alliance	A.751
Tamarix spp. Semi-natural Temporarily Flooded Shrubland Alliance	Salt-cedar species Semi-natural Temporarily Flooded Shrubland Alliance	A.842
Varilla texana - Castela erecta Shrubland Alliance	Saladillo - Amargosa Shrubland Alliance	A.1910
- *Viguiera stenoloba - Bernardia obovata / Chamaesyce* sp. Shrubland	- Skeletonleaf Goldeneye - Desert Myrtle-croton / Sandmat species Shrubland	CEGL004603
- *Zanthoxylum fagara - Forestiera angustifolia - Diospyros texana* Shrubland	- Lime Prickly-ash - Texas Swamp-privet - Texas Persimmon Shrubland	CEGL004615

Table 3. NVC Herbaceous and Sparse Vegetation Alliances and Plant Associations Identified as Potentially Occurring within the AMIS Vegetation Inventory Project Area

NVC Alliance and/or Association	Common Name	Element Code
Adiantum capillus-veneris Saturated Herbaceous Alliance	Southern Maidenhair Saturated Herbaceous Alliance	A.1683
Aristida purpurea Herbaceous Alliance	Purple Threeawn Herbaceous Alliance	A.2570
Arundo donax Temporarily Flooded Herbaceous Alliance	Giant Reed Temporarily Flooded Herbaceous Alliance	A.1339
- Arundo donax Break Herbaceous Vegetation	- Giant Reed Break Herbaceous Vegetation	CEGL00xxxx
Bothriochloa barbinodis Herbaceous Alliance	Cane Beardgrass Herbaceous Alliance	A.1209
- Bothriochloa barbinodis Herbaceous Vegetation	- Cane Beardgrass Herbaceous Vegetation	CEGL005323
Bouteloua curtipendula Herbaceous Alliance	Sideoats Grama Herbaceous Alliance	A.1244
- Bouteloua curtipendula - Bouteloua (eriopoda, gracilis) Herbaceous Vegetation	- Sideoats Grama – (Black Grama, Blue Grama) Herbaceous Vegetation	CEGL002250
Bouteloua gracilis Herbaceous Alliance	Blue Grama Herbaceous Alliance	A.1282
- Bouteloua gracilis - Bouteloua curtipendula Herbaceous Vegetation	- Blue Grama – Sideoats Grama Herbaceous Vegetation	CEGL001754
- Bouteloua gracilis - Bouteloua hirsuta Herbaceous Vegetation	- Blue Grama – Hairy Grama Herbaceous Vegetation	CEGL001755
- Bouteloua gracilis – Buchloe dactyloides Herbaceous Vegetation	- Blue Grama – Buffalograss Herbaceous Vegetation	CEGL001756
Bouteloua hirsuta Herbaceous Alliance	Hairy Grama Herbaceous Alliance	A.1285
- Bouteloua hirsuta - Bouteloua curtipendula Herbaceous Vegetation	- Hairy Grama – Sideoats Grama Herbaceous Vegetation	CEGL001764
Cenchrus (Pennisetum) ciliaris(e) Herbaceous Alliance	Buffelgrass Herbaceous Alliance	A.1211
- Cenchrus ciliaris Semi-natural Herbaceous Vegetation	- Buffelgrass Semi-natural Herbaceous Vegetation	CEGL00xxxx
Cladium mariscus ssp. jamaicense Seasonally Flooded Temperate Herbaceous Alliance	Jamaica Swamp Sawgrass Seasonally Flooded Temperate Herbaceous Alliance	A.1369
Cynodon dactylon Herbaceous Alliance	Bermudagrass Herbaceous Alliance	A.1279
Eleocharis palustris Temporarily Flooded Herbaceous Alliance	Common Sp kerush Temporarily Flooded Herbaceous Alliance	A.1342
- Eleocharis spp. Herbaceous Vegetation	- Sp kerush Species Herbaceous Vegetation	CEGL00xxxx
Eragrostis lehmanniana Semi-natural Herbaceous Alliance	Lehmann's Lovegrass Semi-natural Herbaceous Alliance	A.2687
Hilaria belangeri – Bouteloua curtipendula Herbaceous Alliance	Curly Mesquite – Sideoats Grama Herbaceous Alliance	A.1214
- Hilaria belangeri – Bouteloua curtipendula Herbaceous Vegetation	- Curly Mesquite – Sideoats Grama Herbaceous Vegetation	CEGL002238
Hydrilla verticillata Permanently Flooded Herbaceous Alliance	Water-Thyme Permanently Flooded Herbaceous Alliance	A.1745
- Hydrilla verticillata Submerged Aquatic Vegetation	- Water-Thyme Submerged Aquatic Vegetation	CEGL00xxxx
Lemna spp. Permanently Flooded Herbaceous Alliance	Duckweed Species Permanently Flooded Herbaceous Alliance	A.1747
Lesquerella (gordonii, ovalifolia) Herbaceous Alliance	Gordon's Bladderpod, Oval-leaf Bladderpod) Herbaceous Alliance	A.1619
- Lesquerella (gordonii, ovalifolia) - Schizachyrium scoparium Herbaceous Vegetation	- (Gordon's Bladderpod, Oval-leaf Bladderpod) - Little Bluestem Herbaceous Vegetation	CEGL004917
Justicia americana Temporarily Flooded Herbaceous Alliance	American Water-willow Temporarily Flooded Herbaceous Alliance	A.1657
- Justicia americana Herbaceous Vegetation	- American Water-willow Herbaceous Vegetation	CEGL004286
- Justicia americana - Bacopa monnieri Edwards Plateau Herbaceous Vegetation	- American Water-willow - Coastal Water-hyssop Edwards Plateau Herbaceous Vegetation	CEGL004926
- Marrubium vulgare Semi-natural Herbaceous Vegetation	- Horehound Semi-natural Herbaceous Vegetation	CEGL00xxxx
Open Cliff Sparsely Vegetated Alliance	Open Cliff Sparsely Vegetated Alliance	A.1836
Panicum obtusum Herbaceous Alliance	Vine-mesquite Herbaceous Alliance	A.1238

13

Table 3. NVC Herbaceous and Sparse Vegetation Alliances and Plant Associations Identified as Potentially Occurring within the AMIS Vegetation Inventory Project Area

NVC Alliance and/or Association	Common Name	Element Code
- Panicum obtusum – Buchloe dactyloides Herbaceous Vegetation	- Vine-mesquite – Buffalograss Herbaceous Vegetation	CEGL001573
- Panicum obtusum – Panicum hallii Herbaceous Vegetation	- Vine-mesquite - Hall's Panicgrass Herbaceous Vegetation	CEGL001575
- Panicum obtusum Herbaceous Vegetation	- Vine-mesquite Herbaceous Vegetation	CEGL002708
Panicum virgatum Temporarily Flooded Herbaceous Alliance	Switchgrass Temporarily Flooded Herbaceous Alliance	A.1343
- Panicum virgatum - Andropogon glomeratus – Cladium mariscus ssp. jamaicense Herbaceous Vegetation	- Switchgrass - Bushy Bluestem – Jamaica Swamp Sawgrass Herbaceous Vegetation	CEGL004928
Phragmites australis Herbaceous Alliance	Common Reed Herbaceous Alliance	A.1196
- Phragmites australis Western North America Temperate Semi-natural Herbaceous Vegetation	- Common Reed Western North America Temperate Semi-natural Herbaceous Vegetation	CEGL001475
Phragmites australis Semipermanently Flooded Herbaceous Alliance	Common Reed Semipermanently Flooded Herbaceous Alliance	A.1431
Phragmites australis Temporarily Flooded Herbaceous Alliance	Common Reed Temporarily Flooded Herbaceous Alliance	A.1345
- Phragmites australis Riverbank Herbaceous Vegetation	- Common Reed Riverbank Herbaceous Vegetation	CEGL004115
- Phragmites australis - Arundo donax Riparian Corridor Herbaceous Vegetation	- Common Reed – Giant Reed Riparian Corridor Herbaceous Vegetation	CEGL00xxxx
- Phragmites australis - Panicum virgatum Herbaceous Vegetation	- Common Reed – Switchgrass Herbaceous Vegetation	CEGL00xxxx
- Phyla nodiflora – Cynodon dactylon – Bacopa monnieri Herbaceous Vegetation	- Turkey Tangle Fogfruit – Bermudagrass – Water Hyssop Herbaceous Vegetation	CEGL00xxxx
- Phyla nodiflora / Nicotiana glauca – Vitex agnus-castus Rock Outcrop Sparse Vegetation	- Turkey Tangle Fogfruit / Tree Tobacco – Lilac Chastetree Rock Outcrop Sparse Wooded Herbaceous Vegetation	CEGL00xxxx
Pleuraphis mutica Herbaceous Alliance	Tobosa Grass Herbaceous Alliance	A.1249
- Pleuraphis mutica – Buchloe dactyloides Herbaceous Vegetation	- Tobosa Grass – Buffalograss Herbaceous Vegetation	CEGL002272
Pleuraphis mutica Intermittently Flooded Herbaceous Alliance	Tobosa Grass Intermittently Flooded Herbaceous Alliance	A.1330
- Pleuraphis mutica - Panicum obtusum Herbaceous Vegetation	- Tobosa Grass – Vine-mesquite Herbaceous Vegetation	CEGL001639
Polygonum spp. (section Persicaria) Seasonally Flooded Herbaceous Alliance	Smartweed species Seasonally Flooded Herbaceous Alliance	A.1881
- Salsola kali Semi-natural Herbaceous Vegetation	- Russian-thistle Herbaceous Vegetation	CEGL00xxxx
Schizachyrium scoparium - Bouteloua curtipendula Herbaceous Alliance	Little Bluestem – Sideoats Grama Herbaceous Alliance	A.1225
- Schizachyrium scoparium - Bouteloua curtipendula – Nassela leucotricha Herbaceous Vegetation	- Little Bluestem – Sideoats Grama – Texas Wintergrass Herbaceous Vegetation	CEGL004070
- Schizachyrium scoparium - Bouteloua curtipendula Western Great Plains Herbaceous Vegetation	- Little Bluestem – Sideoats Grama Western Great Plains Herbaceous Vegetation	CEGL001594
Schoenoplectus americanus Semipermanently Flooded Herbaceous Alliance	Chairmaker's Bulrush Semipermanently Flooded Herbaceous Alliance	A.1432
Schoenoplectus californicus Semipermanently Flooded Herbaceous Alliance	Giant Bulrush Semipermanently Flooded Herbaceous Alliance	A.1171
- Schoenoplectus californicus Gulf Coast Herbaceous Vegetation	- Giant Bulrush Gulf Coast Herbaceous Vegetation	CEGL008464
- Schoenoplectus californicus Herbaceous Vegetation	- Giant Bulrush Herbaceous Vegetation	CEGL00xxxx
Schoenoplectus pungens Semipermanently Flooded Herbaceous Alliance	Common Threesquare Semipermanently Flooded Herbaceous Alliance	A.1433
Sorghum halepense Semi-natural Herbaceous Alliance	Johnson Grass Semi-natural Herbaceous Alliance	A.2020
- Sorghum halepense - (Amaranthus palmeri) Semi-natural Herbaceous Vegetation	- Johnson Grass - (Palmer's Amaranth) Semi-natural Herbaceous Vegetation	CEGL005324

Table 3. NVC Herbaceous and Sparse Vegetation Alliances and Plant Associations Identified as Potentially Occurring within the AMIS Vegetation Inventory Project Area

NVC Alliance and/or Association	Common Name	Element Code
Sporobolus cryptandrus Herbaceous Alliance	Sand Dropseed Herbaceous Alliance	A.1252
- *Sporobolus cryptandrus - Schizachyrium scoparium - Bouteloua curtipendula* Herbaceous Vegetation	- Sand Dropseed - Little Bluestem - Sideoats Grama Herbaceous Vegetation	CEGL005031
Sporobolus wrightii Saturated Herbaceous Alliance	Big Alkali Sacaton Saturated Herbaceous Vegetation	A.1435
- *Sporobolus wrightii* Herbaceous Vegetation	- Big Alkali Sacaton Herbaceous Vegetation	CEGL002232
- *Sporobolus wrightii - Panicum obtusum* Herbaceous Vegetation	- Big Alkali Sacaton - Vine-mesquite Herbaceous Vegetation	CEGL001486
Typha domingensis Semipermanently Flooded Tropical Herbaceous Alliance	Southern Cattail Semipermanently Flooded Tropical Herbaceous Alliance	A.1175
- *Typha domingensis – Colacasia esculenta* Semipermanently Flooded Herbaceous Vegetation	- Southern Cattail – Asian Taro Semipermanently Flooded Herbaceous Vegetation	CEGL00xxxx

15#

Literature Cited

Austin, M.P. and P.C. Heyligers. 1989. Vegetation survey design for conservation: gradsect sampling of forests in northeastern New South Wales, Biological Conservation. 50:13-32.

Grossman, D.H., D. Faber-Langendoen, A.S. Weakley, M. Anderson, P. Bourgeron, R. Crawford, K. Goodin, S. Landaal, K. Metzler, K. Patterson, M. Pyne, M. Reid, and L. Sneddon. 1998. International classification of ecological communities: Terrestrial Vegetation of the United States. Volume I. The National Vegetation Classification System: development, status, and applications. The Nature Conservancy. Arlington, VA.

Larson, D. 2002. Preliminary identification of vegetative structure of Amistad National Recreation Area. Personal Communication to Dr. Bill Reid, Chihuahuan Desert Network Coordinator.

Lea, Chris. 2009. Preliminary evaluation of the TPWD-Poole (2004) dataset in reference to classification plot replacement. NPS-USGS National Vegetation Inventory Project Vegetation Ecologist. Denver, CO.

National Park Service. 2010. The Chihuahuan Desert Network. Accessed online at: http://science.nature.nps.gov/im/units/chdn/Parks.cfm.

_____. 2006. Draft General Management Plan / Environmental Assessment. Amistad National Recreation Area, Val Verde County, Texas. Denver, CO.

_____. Amistad National Recreation Area. 2010. Vegetation inventory study plan for Amistad National Recreation Area. J.D. Von Loh and D.R. Cogan. Natural Resource Report NPS/CHDN/NRR-2010/211. National Park Service, Fort Collins, CO.

NatureServe Explorer. 2010. An Online Encyclopedia of Life. Accessed online at: www.natureserve.org/explorer.

Poole, J.M. 2004. An Inventory of the Vascular Plants at Amistad National Recreation Area. Wildlife Diversity Program, Texas Parks and Wildlife Department. Austin, TX.

Poole, J.M. and L.K. Hedges. 1999. Devils River State Natural Area – baseline vegetation study. Texas Parks and Wildlife Department. Austin, TX.

Texas Parks and Wildlife Department, Texas Natural Heritage Program. 1995. Biological Survey of Lake Amistad Recreation Site. Final Report. Texas Parks and Wildlife Department, Austin, TX.

_____. 2009. Web site accessed online at: http://www.tpwd.state.tx.us.

U.S. Department of Agriculture, Natural Resources Conservation Service (USDA, NRCS). 2001. PLANTS Database. Retrieved November 2001, accessed online at: http://plants.usda.gov/home_page.html.

——— Soil Conservation Service. 1982. Soil Survey, Val Verde County, Texas. In cooperation with: Texas Agricultural Experiment Station and Val Verde County Commissioners Court. Austin, TX.

U.S. Department of Homeland Security (DHS). 2008. Environmental Assessment for the Proposed Construction, Operation, and Maintenance of Tactical Infrastructure. U.S. Border Patrol. Del Rio Sector, TX.

Von Loh, J.D. and D.R. Cogan. 2010. Vegetation inventory study plan for Amistad National Recreation Area. Natural Resource Report NPS/CHDN/NRR-2010/211. National Park Service, Fort Collins, CO.

Worthington, R. D. 2002. Preliminary inventory of the flora of Amistad National Recreation Area and surrounding area, south-central Val Verde County, Texas; second working draft. Floristic Inventories of the Southwest Program, El Paso, TX.

Appendix 1: Plant Species List for AMIS

Comprehensive list of plant species observed at AMIS, organized alphabetically by family, and based on field surveys from 1993 to 2004.

(Sources: (1) Poole, J. M. 2004. An inventory of the vascular plants at Amistad National Recreation Area. Texas Natural Heritage Program. (2) 1995. Biological survey of Lake Amistad Recreational Site: Final Report. Texas Natural Heritage Program. Resource Protection Division. Texas Parks and Wildlife Department. 3000 South Interstate 35, Suite 100, Austin, TX 78704.)

Scientific Name	Common Name
Acanthaceae	*Acanthaceae*
Carlowrightia texana	Texas wrightwort
Carlowrightia torreyana	Torrey's wrightwort
Dyschoriste linearis	narrowleaf dyschoriste
Justicia americana	American waterwillow
Justicia wrightii	Wright's justicia
Nomaphila stricta	temple plant
Ruellia corzoi	Corzo's wild petunia
Ruellia davisiorum	Rio Grande wild petunia
Ruellia humilis	fringeleaf wild petunia
Ruellia metziae	Metz's wild petunia
Ruellia nudiflora var. nudiflora	violet wild petunia
Ruellia nudiflora var. runyonii	Runyon's wild petunia
Ruellia occidentalis	western wild petunia
Ruellia parryi	Parry's wild petunia
Siphonoglossa pilosella	hairy tubetongue
Yeatesia platystegia	Montell bractspike
Agavaceae	*Agavaceae*
Agave americana	century plant
Agave lechuguilla	lechuguilla
Hesperaloe parviflora	red yucca
Yucca constricta	Buckley yucca
Yucca reverchonii	San Angelo yucca
Yucca rostrata	Thompson yucca
Yucca rupicola	Texas yucca
Yucca thompsoniana	Thompson yucca
Yucca torreyi	Torrey yucca
Yucca treculeana	Don Quixote's lace
Amaranthaceae	*Amaranthaceae*
Alternanthera caracasana	mat chaff-flower
Amaranthus blitoides	prostrate pigweed
Amaranthus crassipes	spreading amaranth
Amaranthus hybridus	green amaranth
Amaranthus palmeri	Palmer's amaranth
Amaranthus scleropoides	bonebract amaranth
Froelichia arizonica	Arizona snakecotton
Froelichia gracilis	slender snakecotton
Gossypianthus lanuginosus var. lanuginosus	woolly cottonflower
Anacardiaceae	*Anacardiaceae*
Pistacia mexicana	Texas pistachio
Rhus microphylla	littleleaf sumac
Rhus trilobata var. trilobata	skunkbush sumac
Rhus virens	evergreen sumac
Rhus virens var. choriophylla	evergreen sumac

Rhus virens var. virens	evergreen sumac
Toxicodendron radicans	poison ivy

Anemiaceae

Anemiaceae

Anemia mexicana	Mexican fern

Apiaceae

Apiaceae

Ammoselinum butleri	Butler's sand parsley
Ammoselinum popei	Pope's sand parsley
Bifora americana	American bifora
Bowlesia incana	hoary bowlesia
Chaerophyllum tainturieri	chervil
Ciclospermum leptophyllum	slimlobe celery
Cicuta maculata	spotted water hemlock
Daucus pusillus	southwestern carrot
Eryngium diffusum	bushy eryngo
Eryngium leavenworthii	Leavenworth's eryngo
Hydrocotyle verticillata	whorled pennywort
Spermolepis inermis	smooth scaleseed
Torilis arvensis	sockbane

Apocynaceae

Apocynaceae

Amsonia longiflora var. salpignantha	trumpet slimpod
Macrosiphonia lanuginosa var. macrosiphon	plateau rocktrumpet

Aristolochiaceae

Aristolochiaceae

Aristolochia coryi	Cory's pipevine

Asclepiadaceae

Asclepiadaceae

Asclepias asperula	spider antelopehorn
Asclepias incarnata	swamp milkweed
Asclepias oenotheroides	longhorn mi kweed
Cynanchum barbigerum	bearded swallowwort
Cynanchum maccartii	MacCart's swallowwort
Cynanchum racemosum var. unifarium	talayote
Funastrum crispum	wavyleaf twinevine
Matelea reticulata	pearl mi kvine
Matelea sagittifolia	arrowleaf milkvine
Sarcostemma cynanchoides ssp. cynanchoides	twinevine

Asteraceae

Asteraceae

Acourtia runcinata	peonia
Ageratina havanensis	shrubby boneset
Amblyolepis setigera	huisache daisy
Ambrosia artemisiifolia	common ragweed
Ambrosia confertiflora	field ragweed
Ambrosia psilostachya	western ragweed
Aphanostephus ramosissimus var. ramosissimus	lazy daisy
Aphanostephus riddellii	Riddell's lazy daisy
Artemisia dracunculus	false tarragon sagewort
Baccharis neglecta	Roosevelt weed
Baccharis salicifolia	seepwillow
Bahia absinthifolia	hairyseed bahia
Baileya multiradiata	desert marigold
Brickellia dentata	gravelbar brickellbush
Brickellia eupatorioides var. chlorolepis	false boneset
Brickellia laciniata	splitleaf brickellbush
Calyptocarpus vialis	straggler daisy
Carduus tenuiflorus	slender bristlethistle
Centaurea americana	American basketflower
Centaurea melitensis	yellow star-thistle
	hairy leastdaisy

Chaetopappa bellidifolia	manyflower leastdaisy
Chaetopappa bellioides	silverpuff
Chaptalia texana	spiny aster
Chloracantha spinosa	damianita
Chrysactinia mexicana	Texas thistle
Cirsium texanum	Turner's cliff thistle
Cirsium turneri	Gregg's eupatorium
Conoclinium greggii	Canadian horseweed
Conyza canadensis	false daisy
Eclipta prostrata	running fleabane
Erigeron colomexicanus	Plains fleabane
Erigeron modestus	white boneset
Eupatorium serotinum	flathead rabbit tobacco
Evax prolifera	roundhead rabbit tobacco
Evax verna	sticky palafoxia
Florestina tripteris	tarbush
Flourensia cernua	Shinner's brickelbush
Flyriella parryi	Coahuila Indian blanket
Gaillardia coahuilensis	slender gaillardia
Gaillardia pinnatifida	Indian blanket
Gaillardia pulchella var. pulchella	rayless gaillardia
Gaillardia suavis	narrowleaf purple everlasting
Gamochaeta falcata	chomonque
Gochnatia hypoleuca	manyray gumweed
Grindelia grandiflora	threadleaf snakeweed
Gutierrezia microcephala	broom snakeweed
Gutierrezia sarothrae	roundleaf snakeweed
Gutierrezia sphaerocephala	tatalencho
Gymnosperma glutinosum	false broomweed
Haploesthes greggii var. texana	pretty sneezeweed
Helenium elegans var. elegans	smallhead sneezeweed
Helenium microcephalum	smallhead sneezeweed
Helenium microcephalum var. microcephalum	smallhead sneezeweed
Helenium microcephalum var. ooclinium	common sunflower
Helianthus annuus	rocky goldaster
Heterotheca fulcrata	camphorweed
Heterotheca subaxillaris	fragrant bitterweed
Hymenoxys odorata	wild lettuce
Lactuca serriola	Coulter's conyza
Laennecia coulteri	dotted gayfeather
Liatris punctata	Texas star
Lindheimera texana	lacy tansyaster
Machaeranthera pinnatifida var. pinnatifida	blackfoot daisy
Melampodium cinereum var. hirtellum	plains blackfoot daisy
Melampodium leucanthum	small palafox
Palafoxia callosa	Texas palafoxia
Palafoxia texana var. texana	lyreleaf parthenium
Parthenium confertum	ragweed parthenium
Parthenium hysterophorus	mariola
Parthenium incanum	crownseed pectis
Pectis angustifolia	narrowleaf rockdaisy
Perityle angustifolia	Lindheimer rockdaisy
Perityle lindheimeri	rock lettuce
Pinaropappus roseus	purple pluchea
Pluchea carolinensis	poreleaf

Scientific name	Common name
Porophyllum scoparium	Jersey cudweed
Pseudognaphalium luteoalbum	cudweed paperflower
Psilostrophe gnaphalioides	hairy paperflower
Psilostrophe tagetina var. cerifera	manystem false dandelion
Pyrrhopappus pauciflorus	Mexican hat
Ratibida columnifera	threadleaf groundsel
Senecio flaccidus var. flaccidus	bush sunflower
Simsia calva	Julia's goldenrod
Solidago juliae	common sowthistle
Sonchus oleraceus	hierba del marrano
Symphyotrichum divaricatum	southwestern annual saltmarsh aster
Symphyotrichum expansum	Plateau nerveray
Tetragonotheca texana	clustered bitterweed
Tetraneuris scaposa var. argyrocaulon	slender greenthread
Thelesperma filifolium	bighead greenthread
Thelesperma megapotamicum	slender greenthread
Thelesperma simplicifolium	needle dogweed
Thymophylla acerosa	woolly dogweed
Thymophylla micropoides	fiveneedle pricklyleaf
Thymophylla pentachaeta	parralena
Thymophylla pentachaeta var. pentachaeta	Texas pricklyleaf
Thymophylla setifolia var. radiata	bristleleaf dogweed
Thymophylla tenuiloba var. tenuiloba	Trecul's bristleleaf dogweed
Thymophylla tenuiloba var. treculii	cowpen daisy
Verbesina encelioides	plateau golden-eye
Viguiera dentata	skeletonleaf goldeneye
Viguiera stenoloba	hairy wedelia
Wedelia texana	cocklebur
Xanthium strumarium	

Berberidaceae

Mahonia trifoliolata	agarita

Bignoniaceae

Chilopsis linearis	desert willow
Tecoma stans	yellow bells

Bixaceae

Amoreuxia wrightii	yellow show

Boraginaceae

Antiphytum heliotropioides	Mexican saucerflower
Cordia podocephala	cluster cordia
Cryptantha mexicana	Mexican cryptantha
Cryptantha micrantha	redroot cryptantha
Cryptantha palmeri	Palmer's cryptantha
Heliotropium confertifolium	leafy heliotrope
Heliotropium curassavicum var. curassavicum	seaside heliotrope
Heliotropium curassavicum var. curassavicum	salt heliotrope
Heliotropium procumbens	foursp ke heliotrope
Heliotropium torreyi	Torrey heliotrope
Lappula occidentalis	flatspine stickseed
Lappula redowskii	flatspine stickseed
Lithospermum incisum	narrowleaf gromwell
Lithospermum matamorense	Mexican navelseed
Lithospermum mirabile	San Antonio stoneseed
Lithospermum parksii	Parks' gromwell
Omphalodes aliena	Mexican navelseed
Tiquilia canescens	woody crinklemat
Tiquilia canescens var. canescens	gray coldenia
Tiquilia mexicana	Mexican coldenia

Brassicaceae	*Brassicaceae*
Brassica juncea	India mustard
Descurainia pinnata	tansy mustard
Draba cuneifolia	wedgeleaf draba
Draba platycarpa	broadpod whitlowwort
Eruca vesicaria ssp. sativa	rocketsalad
Lepidium austrinum	hairy peppergrass
Lepidium lasiocarpum var. wrightii	hairypod peppergrass
Lepidium virginicum	smooth pepperweed
Lesquerella argyraea	silver bladderpod
Lesquerella fendleri	Fendler's bladderpod
Lesquerella gordonii	Gordon bladderpod
Lesquerella gracilis	white bladderpod
Lesquerella purpurea	rose bladderpod
Lesquerella recurvata	slender bladderpod
Nerisyrenia camporum	mesa greggia
Rorippa nasturtium-aquaticum	watercress
Rorippa teres	southern marsh yellowcress
Sisymbrium irio	London rocket
Streptanthus platycarpus	broadpod twistflower

Bromeliaceae	*Bromeliaceae*
Tillandsia recurvata	ballmoss

Cactaceae	*Cactaceae*
Ancistrocactus brevihamatus	short-spined fishhook cactus
Ancistrocactus tobuschii	Tobusch fishhook cactus
Ariocarpus fissuratus	living rock cactus
Coryphantha echinus var. echinus	sea-urchin cactus
Coryphantha pottsiana	Runyon's pincushion cactus
Coryphantha sulcata	grooved nipple cactus
Coryphantha tuberculosa	cob cactus
Echinocactus horizonthalonius	eagle claw cactus
Echinocactus texensis	horse-crippler
Echinocereus coccineus var. paucispinus	Texas claret-cup cactus
Echinocereus enneacanthus var. enneacanthus	strawberry cactus
Echinocereus pectinatus var. wenigeri	Langtry rainbow cactus
Echinocereus stramineus	strawberry cactus
Epithelantha micromeris	common button cactus
Ferocactus hamatacanthus var. hamatacanthus	giant fishhook-cactus
Glandulicactus uncinatus var. wrightii	eagle-claw cactus
Hamatocactus bicolor	twisted-rib cactus
Mammillaria heyderi var. heyderi	Heyder's pincushion cactus
Mammillaria lasiacantha	golf ball cactus
Mammillaria prolifera var. texana	hair-covered cactus
Neolloydia conoidea	Texas cone cactus
Opuntia atrispina	black-and-yellow spined prickly pear
Opuntia engelmannii var. lindheimeri	Texas prickly pear
Opuntia leptocaulis	Christmas cholla
Opuntia macrocentra var. macrocentra	long-spined purplish prickly pear
Opuntia phaeacantha	brown-spined prickly pear
Opuntia schottii var. schottii	Schott's dog cholla
Opuntia X subarmata	prickly pear

Campanulaceae	*Campanulaceae*
Lobelia berlandieri var. brachypoda	blue lobelia
Lobelia cardinalis	cardinal flower

Triodanis coloradoensis	Colorado Venus' looking-glass
Triodanis leptocarpa	slimpod Venus' looking-glass
Triodanis perfoliata	Venus' looking-glass

Capparaceae

Koeberlinia spinosa	allthorn
Polanisia dodecandra ssp. trachysperma	clammyweed

Caryophyllaceae

Arenaria benthamii	Bentham sandwort
Paronychia jamesii	James nailwort
Silene antirrhina	sleepy catchfly

Celastraceae

Mortonia sempervirens	rough mortonia
Schaefferia cuneifolia	desert yaupon

Chenopodiaceae

Atriplex canescens	fourwing saltbush
Chenopodium berlandieri var. berlandieri	pitseed goosefoot
Chenopodium incanum	mealy goosefoot
Chenopodium pratericola	thickleaf goosefoot
Kochia scoparia	Mexican fireweed
Salsola tragus	Russian thistle
Suaeda moquinii	quelite salado

Commelinaceae

Commelina erecta	erect dayflower
Tinantia anomala	false dayflower
Tradescantia brevifolia	Trans-Pecos spiderwort
Tradescantia occidentalis	prairie spiderwort

Convolvulaceae

Bonamia repens	creeping petrogenia
Convolvulus arvensis	field bindweed
Convolvulus equitans	hoary bindweed
Dichondra micrantha	Asian ponysfoot
Evolvulus alsinoides var. angustifolius	ojo de vibora
Evolvulus nuttallianus	hairy evolvulus
Evolvulus sericeus	silky evolvulus
Ipomoea cordatotriloba	tievine
Ipomoea cordatotriloba var. cordatotriloba	tievine
Ipomoea costellata	crestrib morning glory
Ipomoea lindheimeri	Lindheimer morning glory
Ipomoea rupicola	cliff morning glory
Ipomoea sagittata	saltmarsh morning glory
Merremia dissecta	Alamovine

Crassulaceae

Sedum wrightii	*Wright's stonecrop*

Cucurbitaceae

Apodanthera undulata	chile coyote
Cucurbita foetidissima	buffalo gourd
Ibervillea lindheimeri	Lindheimer globeberry
Ibervillea tenuisecta	slimlobe globeberry
Melothria pendula	creeping cucumber

Cupressaceae

Juniperus ashei	Ashe juniper
Juniperus pinchotii	redberry juniper

Cuscutaceae

Cuscuta exaltata	oak dodder
Cuscuta indecora	bigseed alfalfa dodder

Cuscuta indecora var. indecora	bigseed alfalfa dodder
Cuscuta indecora var. neuropetala	bigseed dodder
Cuscuta pentagona var. glabrior	bushclover dodder
Cuscuta pentagona var. pubescens	bushclover dodder

Cyperaceae

Carex microdonta	littletooth sedge
Carex planostachys	cedar sedge
Cladium mariscus ssp. jamaicense	Jamaica sawgrass
Cyperus acuminatus	taperleaf flatsedge
Cyperus elegans	sticky flatsedge
Cyperus ochraceus	pond flatsedge
Cyperus odoratus	fragrant flatsedge
Cyperus squarrosus	bearded flatsedge
Eleocharis cellulosa	Gulf Coast spikesedge
Eleocharis geniculata	annual spikesedge
Eleocharis interstincta	knotted spikerush
Eleocharis montevidensis	sand spikesedge
Eleocharis palmeri	sand spikerush
Eleocharis palustris	large sp kesedge
Eleocharis rostellata	tussock spikesedge
Fimbristylis vahlii	Vahl's fimbry
Fuirena simplex	porcupine sedge
Rhynchospora colorata	whitetop sedge
Rhynchospora nivea	showy whitetop
Schoenoplectus americanus	chairmaker's bulrush
Schoenoplectus californicus	California bulrush
Schoenoplectus pungens	American bulrush
Schoenoplectus tabernaemontani	softstem bulrush

Ebenaceae

Diospyros texana	Texas persimmon

Ephedraceae

Ephedra antisyphilitica	clap-weed, popote
Ephedra aspera	boundary ephedra
Ephedra pedunculata	vine joint-for

Equisetaceae

Equisetum hyemale var. affine	scouring-rush horsetail
Equisetum laevigatum	smooth scouring-rush

Euphorbiaceae

Acalypha monostachya	creeping copperleaf
Acalypha phleoides	Lindheimer copperleaf
Argythamnia neomexicana	New Mexico wildmercury
Bernardia myricifolia	brush myrtlecroton
Bernardia obovata	desert myrtlecroton
Chamaesyce acuta	pointed spurge
Chamaesyce albomarginata	whitemargin spurge
Chamaesyce angusta	narrowleaf spurge
Chamaesyce cinerascens	shy spurge
Chamaesyce glyptosperma	ridgeseed spurge
Chamaesyce hyssopifolia	hyssop-leaf spurge
Chamaesyce maculata	spotted sandmat
Chamaesyce prostrata	prostrate spurge
Chamaesyce serpens	smooth matspurge
Croton capitatus var. lindheimeri	Lindheimer's hogwort
Croton dioicus	grassland croton

Croton fruticulosus	bush croton
Croton incanus	vara blanca
Croton lindheimerianus var. lindheimerianus	Tharp croton
Croton monanthogynus	oneseed croton
Croton pottsii	leatherweed croton
Croton pottsii var. pottsii	
Euphorbia antisyphilitica	candelilla
Euphorbia cyathophora	wild poinsettia
Euphorbia davidii	toothed spurge
Euphorbia longicruris	longhorn spurge
Euphorbia peplidion	low euphorbia
Euphorbia spathulata	warty spurge
Jatropha dioica var. dioica	leatherstem
Leptopus phyllanthoides	maidenbush
Phyllanthus polygonoides	knotweed leafflower
Ricinus communis	castorbean
Stillingia treculiana	Trecul stillingia
Tragia amblyodonta	dogtooth noseburn
Tragia ramosa	catnip noseburn
Triadica sebifera	Chinese tallow tree

Fabaceae

Fabaceae

Acacia angustissima var. chisosiana	Chisos prairie acacia
Acacia angustissima var. hirta	prairie acacia
Acacia berlandieri	guajillo
Acacia constricta	white thorn acacia
Acacia farnesiana	huisache
Acacia greggii	catclaw acacia
Acacia neovernicosa	stickleaf acacia
Acacia rigidula	blackbrush
Acacia roemeriana	Roemer acacia
Acacia wrightii	Wright acacia
Amorpha fruticosa	bastard indigo
Astragalus nuttallianus var. austrinus	small flowered milkvetch
Astragalus wrightii	Wright locoweed
Bauhinia lunarioides	Texas bauhinia
Calliandra conferta	fairy duster
Cercis canadensis	eastern redbud
Cercis canadensis var. texensis	redbud
Dalea aurea	golden dalea
Dalea bicolor var. argyrea	silver dalea
Dalea compacta var. pubescens	showy prairie clover
Dalea formosa	feather dalea
Dalea frutescens	black dalea
Dalea nana	dwarf dalea
Dalea neomexicana	New Mexico dalea
Dalea pogonathera var. pogonathera	bearded dalea
Dalea pogonathera var. walkerae	Wa ker's bearded dalea
Desmanthus glandulosus	glandular bundleflower
Desmanthus illinoensis	Illinois bundleflower
Desmanthus obtusus	bundleflower
Desmanthus velutinus	hairy bundleflower
Desmanthus virgatus	wild tantan
Eysenhardtia texana	Texas kidneywood
Galactia texana	Texas mi kpea
Glottidium vesicarium	bagpod
Hoffmannseggia glauca	sicklepod rushpea
Hoffmannseggia oxycarpa	sharppod rushpea
Indigofera lindheimeriana	creek indigo

Leucaena retusa	golden ball leadtree
Lupinus texensis	Texas bluebonnet
Medicago arabica	spotted bur-clover
Melilotus indicus	annual yellow sourclover
Mimosa aculeaticarpa var. biuncifera	catclaw mimosa
Mimosa borealis	fragrant mimosa
Mimosa texana	Texas mimosa
Neptunia pubescens var. microcarpa	tropical puff
Parkinsonia aculeata	retama
Parkinsonia texana var. texana	Texas paloverde
Pediomelum humile	Rydberg scurfpea
Prosopis glandulosa	honey mesquite
Prosopis glandulosa var. glandulosa	mesquite
Prosopis glandulosa var. torreyana	western honey mesquite
Rhynchosia senna var. texana	Texas snoutbean
Senna bauhinioides	shrubby senna
Senna lindheimeriana	Lindheimer senna
Senna pumilio	dwarf senna
Senna roemeriana	twoleaf senna
Sophora secundiflora	Texas mountain laurel
Vicia leavenworthii	Leavenworth's vetch

Fagaceae — *Fagaceae*

Quercus fusiformis	Plateau liveoak
Quercus gravesii	Graves oak
Quercus mohriana	Mohrs shin oak
Quercus polymorpha	Mexican white oak
Quercus vaseyana	Vasey oak

Fouquieriaceae — *Fouquieriaceae*

Fouquieria splendens — ocotillo

Fumariaceae — *Fumariaceae*

Corydalis curvisiliqua ssp. curvisiliqua	scrambled eggs
Corydalis micrantha ssp. texensis	Texan fumewort

Gentianaceae — *Gentianaceae*

Centaurium beyrichii	mountain pink
Centaurium calycosum	rosita
Eustoma exaltatum	prairie gentian
Sabatia campestris	Texas star

Geraniaceae — *Geraniaceae*

Erodium cicutarium	alfilaria
Erodium texanum	Texas stork's bill

Hydrangeaceae — *Hydrangeaceae*

Fendlera wrightii — cliff Fendlerbush

Hydrocharitaceae — *Hydrocharitaceae*

Hydrilla verticillata — hydrilla

Hydrophyllaceae — *Hydrophyllaceae*

Nama havardii	Havard's fiddleleaf
Nama hispidum	rough nama
Nama jamaicense	fiddleleaf nama
Nama parvifolium	small leaf fiddlehead
Phacelia congesta	bluecurls
Phacelia patuliflora var. teucriifolia	sand phacelia

Iridaceae — *Iridaceae*

Sisyrinchium biforme	wiry blue-eyed grass
Sisyrinchium chilense	swordleaf blue-eyed grass

Juglandaceae — *Juglandaceae*

Carya illinoinensis — pecan

Juglans microcarpa	little walnut

Juncaceae

Juncus bufonius	toad rush
Juncus interior	inland rush
Juncus nodosus	jointed rush
Juncus torreyi	Torrey rush

Krameriaceae

Krameria erecta	littleleaf ratany
Krameria grayi	white ratany
Krameria lanceolata	trailing ratany
Krameria ramosissima	calderona

Lamiaceae

Hedeoma acinoides	annual pennyroyal
Hedeoma drummondii	lemoncillo
Hedeoma nana	dwarf hedeoma
Hedeoma serpyllifolia	false pennyroyal
Marrubium vulgare	horehound
Monarda citriodora	lemon beebalm
Monarda punctata	spotted beebalm
Physostegia correllii	Correll's false dragonhead
Salvia ballotiflora	shrubby blue sage
Salvia dolichantha	cluster sage
Salvia farinacea var. farinacea	mealy sage
Salvia reflexa	lanceleaf sage
Salvia roemeriana	cedar sage
Salvia texana	Texas sage
Scutellaria drummondii	Drummond's skullcap
Scutellaria drummondii var. edwardsiana	Drummond's skullcap
Scutellaria texana	Texas skullcap
Teucrium canadense	American germander

Lemnaceae

Lemna valdiviana	pale duckweed

Lentibulariaceae

Utricularia gibba	conespur bladderwort

Liliacae

Allium drummondii	Drummond wild onion
Allium perdulce var. sperryi	Sperry's onion
Cooperia drummondii	cebolleta
Cooperia pedunculata	giant rainlily
Dasylirion texanum	sotol
Echeandia flavescens	yellow crag-lily
Nolina texana	beargrass
Nothoscordum bivalve	crow-poison
Schoenocaulon texanum	green lily

Linaceae

Linum berlandieri var. filifolium	Berlandier's yellow flax
Linum rigidum	stiffstem flax
Linum rupestre	rock flax
Linum usitatissimum	common flax
Linum vernale	spring flax

Loasaceae

Cevallia sinuata	stinging cevallia
Eucnide bartonioides	rock nettle
Mentzelia albescens	wavyleaf mentzelia
Mentzelia multiflora	Adonis blazing star
Mentzelia oligosperma	stickleaf, chicken-thief

Loganiaceae	*Loganiaceae*
Mitreola petiolata	hornpod

Lythraceae	*Lythraceae*
Ammannia coccinea	valley redstem
Lythrum californicum	California loosestrife
Nesaea longipes	stalkflower

Malpighiaceae	*Malpighiaceae*
Aspicarpa hyssopifolia	hyssophead aspleaf
Galphimia angustifolia	narrowleaf thryallis
Janusia gracilis	slender janusia

Malvaceae	*Malvaceae*
Abutilon fruticosum	Texas indianmallow
Abutilon incanum	pelotazo
Abutilon parvulum	little leaf abutilon
Abutilon wrightii	Wright's Indianmallow
Allowissadula holosericea	velvet leaf mallow
Callirhoe involucrata	purple poppymallow
Callirhoe leiocarpa	tall poppymallow
Herissantia crispa	netvein herissantia
Hibiscus coulteri	yellow desert-mallow
Hibiscus martianus	heartleaf hibiscus
Malva parviflora	cheeseweed mallow
Malvastrum coromandelianum	threelobe falsemallow
Meximalva filipes	violet sida
Sida abutifolia	creeping yellow sida
Sida longipes	stalkflower sida
Sphaeralcea angustifolia	narrowleaf globe mallow
Sphaeralcea hastulata	spear globemallow

Marsileaceae	*Marsileaceae*
Marsilea vestita	narrowleaf pepperwort
Marsilea vestita ssp. vestita	narrowleaf pepperwort

Meliaceae	*Meliaceae*
Melia azedarach	Chinaberry

Menispermeaceae	*Menispermeaceae*
Cocculus carolinus	Carolina snailseed

Moraceae	*Moraceae*
Morus alba	white mulberry

Najadaceae	*Najadaceae*
Najas guadalupensis	Guadalupe water nymph
Najas marina	spiny water nymph

Nyctaginaceae	*Nyctaginaceae*
Acleisanthes anisophylla	oblique-leaf trumpets
Acleisanthes crassifolia	Texas trumpets
Acleisanthes longiflora	angel trumpets
Acleisanthes wrightii	Wright's trumpets
Allionia incarnata	trailing four-o'clock
Boerhavia coccinea	scarlet spiderling
Boerhavia linearifolia	narrowleaf spiderling
Cyphomeris gypsophiloides	red cyphomeris
Mirabilis a bida	white four-o'clock
Nyctaginia capitata	scarlet muskflower

Nymphaeaceae	*Nymphaeaceae*
Nuphar lutea	*yellow pond-lily*

Oleaceae	*Oleaceae*
Forestiera angustifolia	narrowleaf elbowbush
Forestiera reticulata	netleaf elbowbush

Fraxinus berlandieriana	Berlandier ash
Fraxinus greggii	Gregg ash
Fraxinus texensis	Texas ash
Fraxinus velutina	velvet ash
Menodora heterophylla	redbud menodora
Menodora longiflora	showy menodora
Menodora scabra	rough menodora

Onagraceae

Onagraceae

Calylophus berlandieri ssp. berlandieri	halfshrub sundrops
Calylophus berlandieri ssp. pinifolius	Berlandier's sundrops
Calylophus hartwegii ssp. hartwegii	Hartweg evening primrose
Calylophus hartwegii ssp. maccartii	MacCart's sundrops
Calylophus hartwegii ssp. pubescens	Hartweg's sundrops
Calylophus tubicula	bush evening primrose
Gaura calcicola	Texas beeblossom
Gaura coccinea	scarlet gaura
Gaura drummondii	Drummond's beeblossom
Gaura mollis	lizardtail gaura
Gaura suffulta	wild honeysuckle
Ludwigia octovalvis	shrubby water primrose
Ludwigia palustris	creeping waterprimrose
Oenothera falfurriae	royal evening primrose
Oenothera kunthiana	Kunth sundrops
Oenothera laciniata	cutleaf evening primrose
Oenothera primiveris	desert evening primrose
Oenothera pubescens	South American evening primrose
Oenothera rosea	rose sundrops
Oenothera speciosa	showy evening primrose
Oenothera triloba	stemless evening primrose

Orchidaceae

Epipactis gigantea

Orchidaceae

chatterbox orchid

Orobanchaceae

Orobanchaceae

Orobanche ludoviciana	Louisiana broomrape
Orobanche multicaulis	spiked broomrape

Oxalidaceae

Oxalidaceae

Oxalis dichondrifolia	ponyfoot woodsorrell
Oxalis drummondii	Drummond woodsorrell
Oxalis stricta	yellow woodsorrell
Oxalis violacea	violet woodsorrell

Papaveraceae

Papaveraceae

Argemone aenea	golden pricklypoppy
Argemone chisosensis	Chisos pricklypoppy
Argemone mexicana	yellow pricklypoppy

Passifloraceae

Passifloraceae

Passiflora affinis	yellow passionflower
Passiflora tenuiloba	slenderlobe passionflower

Pedaliaceae

Proboscidea louisianica

Pedaliaceae

Devil's claw

Phytolaccaceae

Rivina humilis

Phytolaccaceae

pigeonberry

Plantaginaceae

Plantaginaceae

Plantago helleri	Heller plantain
Plantago hookeriana	Hooker's plantain

Plantago major	common plantain
Plantago rhodosperma	redseed plantain

Platanaceae
Platanus occidentalis	sycamore

Poaceae
Andropogon glomeratus	bushy bluestem
Aristida adscensionis	sixweeks threeawn
Aristida purpurea var. longiseta	red threeawn
Aristida purpurea var. nealleyi	Nealley threeawn
Aristida purpurea var. purpurea	purple threeawn
Aristida purpurea var. wrightii	Wright's threeawn
Arundo donax	giant cane
Avena fatua	wild oat
Bothriochloa barbinodis	cane bluestem
Bothriochloa hybrida	hybrid bluestem
Bothriochloa ischaemum var. songarica	yellow bluestem
Bothriochloa laguroides ssp. torreyana	silver beardgrass
Bouteloua aristidoides	needle grama
Bouteloua barbata	sixweeks grama
Bouteloua curtipendula	sideoats grama
Bouteloua gracilis	blue grama
Bouteloua hirsuta	hairy grama
Bouteloua rigidiseta	Texas grama
Bouteloua trifida	red grama
Bromus catharticus	rescue grass
Bromus rubens	red brome
Buchloe dactyloides	buffalograss
Cenchrus ciliaris	buffelgrass
Cenchrus echinatus	southern sandbur
Cenchrus myosuroides	big sandbur
Cenchrus spinifex	common sandbur
Chloris crinita	false Rhodesgrass
Chloris cucullata	hooded windmill grass
Chloris pluriflora	multiflower false Rhodes grass
Chloris verticillata	tumble windmill grass
Chloris X subdolichostachya	shortsp ke windmill grass
Cynodon dactylon	Bermuda grass
Dasyochloa pulchella	fluffgrass
Dichanthelium acuminatum var. acuminatum	woolly panicgrass
Dichanthelium pedicellatum	cedar panicgrass
Dichanthium annulatum	Kleberg bluestem
Digitaria californica	Arizona cottontop
Digitaria cognata	fall witchgrass
Digitaria hitchcockii	shortleaf cottontop
Echinochloa colona	jungle-rice
Echinochloa muricata	rough barnyard grass
Echinochloa walteri	coast cockspur grass
Eleusine indica	Indian goosegrass
Elymus canadensis	Canada wildrye
Elymus virginicus	Virginia wildrye
Enneapogon desvauxii	feather pappusgrass
Eragrostis barrelieri	Mediterranean lovegrass
Eragrostis cilianensis	stinkgrass
Eragrostis curtipedicellata	gummy lovegrass
Eragrostis intermedia	Plains lovegrass
Eragrostis lehmanniana	Lehmann's lovegrass
Eragrostis palmeri	Rio Grande lovegrass

Eragrostis pectinacea	spreading lovegrass
Eriochloa sericea	silky cupgrass
Erioneuron pilosum	hairy tridens
Hemarthria altissima	limpograss
Heteropogon contortus	tanglehead
Hilaria belangeri	curlymesquite
Leersia oryzoides	rice cutgrass
Leptochloa dubia	green sprangletop
Leptochloa fascicularis	salt sprangletop
Leptochloa mucronata	red sprangletop
Leptochloa uninervia	Mexican sprangletop
Leptoloma cognatum	fall witchgrass
Limnodea arkansana	Ozarkgrass
Lolium perenne	perennial ryegrass
Melica montezumae	Montezuma melic
Melica nitens	threeflower melic
Muhlenbergia lindheimeri	Lindheimer muhly
Muhlenbergia parviglumis	longawn muhly
Muhlenbergia porteri	bush muhly
Nassella leucotricha	Texas wintergrass
Panicum antidotale	blue panicum
Panicum hallii var. filipes	filly panicum
Panicum hallii var. hallii	Hall's panicum
Panicum obtusum	vine mesquite
Panicum virgatum	switchgrass
Pappophorum bicolor	pink pappusgrass
Paspalum dilatatum	Dallisgrass
Paspalum distichum	knotgrass
Paspalum pubiflorum	hairyseed paspalum
Paspalum urvillei	Vaseygrass
Phalaris caroliniana	Carolina canarygrass
Phragmites australis	giant reed
Pleuraphis mutica	tobosagrass
Poa annua	annual bluegrass
Poa bigelovii	Bigelow bluegrass
Polypogon monspeliensis	rabbit-foot grass
Polypogon viridis	water bentgrass
Schizachyrium scoparium	little bluestem
Setaria grisebachii	Grisebach bristlegrass
Setaria leucopila	Plains bristlegrass
Setaria parviflora	knotroot bristlegrass
Setaria pumila	yellow bristlegrass
Setaria ramiseta	Rio Grande bristlegrass
Setaria reverchonii	Reverchon bristlegrass
Setaria scheelei	southwestern bristlegrass
Setaria texana	Texas bristlegrass
Setaria verticillata	hooked bristlegrass
Setaria viridis	green bristlegrass
Sorghum halepense	Johnsongrass
Sphenopholis obtusata	prairie wedgescale
Sporobolus compositus	tall dropseed
Sporobolus coromandelianus	whorled dropseed
Sporobolus cryptandrus	sand dropseed
Sporobolus wrightii	big sacaton
Stenotaphrum secundatum	St. Augustine grass
Trichoneura elegans	Silveus' grass
Tridens albescens	white tridens
Tridens eragrostoides	lovegrass tridens
Tridens muticus var. muticus	slim tridens
Tridens texanus	Texas tridens
Trisetum interruptum	prairie trisetum
	browntop panicum

Urochloa fasciculata	common sixweeksgrass
Vulpia octoflora	coast agropogon
X Agropogon littoralis	

Polemoniaceae

Gilia incisa	cutleaf gilia
Gilia insignis	marked gilia
Gilia rigidula	blue gilia
Gilia rigidula ssp. acerosa	blue gilia
Gilia rigidula ssp. rigidula	blue gilia

Polygalaceae

Polygala alba	white mi kwort
Polygala lindheimeri var. lindheimeri	purple milkwort
Polygala lindheimeri var. parvifolia	rock milkwort
Polygala macradenia	glandleaf milkwort
Polygala ovatifolia	eggleaf milkwort
Polygala palmeri	Palmer's mi kwort
Polygala scoparioides	broom milkwort

Polygonaceae

Eriogonum havardii	Havard's wild buckwheat
Eriogonum longifolium	longleaf buckwheat
Eriogonum multiflorum	heartsepal buckwheat
Polygonum hydropiperoides	swamp smartweed
Polygonum pensylvanicum	Pennsylvania smartweed
Polygonum persicaria	lady's thumb
Polygonum punctatum	water smartweed
Rumex altissimus	pale dock
Rumex crispus	curly dock
Rumex maritimus	golden dock
Rumex stenophyllus	narrowleaf dock
Rumex violascens	violet dock

Portulacaceae

Portulaca oleracea	common purslane
Portulaca pilosa	shaggy portulaca
Talinum aurantiacum	orange flameflower

Potamogetonaceae

Potamogeton illinoensis	Illinois pondweed
Stuckenia pectinata	fennel-leaf pondweed

Primulaceae

Anagallis arvensis	scarlet pimpernel
Samolus ebracteatus ssp. cuneatus	largeflower brookweed
Samolus valerandi ssp. parviflorus	smallflower brookwood

Pteridaceae

Adiantum capillus-veneris	southern maidenhair
Argyrochosma microphylla	littleleaf cliffbrake
Astrolepis cochisensis	Cochise scaly cloakfern
Astrolepis integerrima	wavyleaf cloakfern
Astrolepis sinuata ssp. sinuata	bu b lipfern
Astrolepis windhamii	Windham's scaly cloakfern
Cheilanthes aemula	Texas lipfern
Cheilanthes alabamensis	Alabama lipfern
Cheilanthes horridula	prickly lipfern
Cheilanthes sinuata	wavy scaly cloakfern
Notholaena copelandii	Copeland cloakfern
Notholaena nealleyi	Neally's cloakfern

Notholaena neglecta	Maxon's cloakfern
Notholaena standleyi	star cloakfern
Pellaea ovata	zigzag cliffbrake

Rafflesiaceae

Pilostyles thurberi	Thurber's stemsucker

Ranunculaceae

Anemone edwardsiana	twoflower anemone
Anemone tuberosa var. texana	tuber anemone
Clematis drummondii	old man's beard
Clematis pitcheri	leatherflower
Delphinium carolinianum ssp. virescens	Carolina larkspur
Delphinium madrense	Sierra Madre larkspur
Delphinium wootonii	Organ Mountain larkspur
Ranunculus sceleratus	blister buttercup

Resedaceae

Oligomeris linifolia	lineleaf whitepuff

Rhamnaceae

Colubrina texensis	hog-plum
Condalia ericoides	javelina bush
Condalia hookeri var. hookeri	brasil
Condalia spathulata	narrowleaf squawbush
Condalia viridis	green squawbush
Condalia warnockii	Warnock's squawbush
Karwinskia humboldtiana	coyotillo
Ziziphus obtusifolia	lotebush

Rosaceae

Prunus minutiflora	Texas almond
Rubus riograndis	Rio Grande dewberry

Rubiaceae

Cephalanthus occidentalis	buttonbush
Galium aparine	cling-on bedstraw
Galium correllii	Correll's bedstraw
Galium microphyllum	bracted bedstraw
Galium proliferum	spreading bedstraw
Galium uncinulatum	sprawling bedstraw
Galium virgatum	wand bedstraw
Hedyotis nigricans	diamondflowers
Houstonia acerosa	needleleaf bluets

Rutaceae

Ptelea trifoliata	skunkbush, wafer ash
Thamnosma texana	Dutchman's breeches
Zanthoxylum hirsutum	tickle-tongue

Salicaceae

Populus deltoides	eastern cottonwood
Salix exigua	coyote willow
Salix gooddingii	Goodding willow
Salix nigra	black willow

Sapindaceae

Sapindus saponaria var. drummondii	western soapberry
Serjania brachycarpa	littlefruit slipplejack
Ungnadia speciosa	Mexican buckeye

Sapotaceae

Sideroxylon lanuginosum ssp. rigidum	coma, gum elastic

Scrophulariaceae

Bacopa monnieri	water hyssop

Buchnera americana	Florida bluehearts
Castilleja lanata	woolly Indian paintbrush
Castilleja rigida	rigid Indian paintbrush
Castilleja sessiliflora	downy Indian paintbrush
Leucophyllum frutescens	cenizo
Leucophyllum minus	Big Bend barometer bush
Leucospora multifida	narrowleaf conobea
Maurandella antirrhiniflora	snapdragon vine
Mecardonia procumbens	baby jump-up
Mimulus glabratus	yellow monkeyflower
Penstemon baccharifolius	baccharisleaf penstemon
Penstemon triflorus	Heller Penstemon
Seymeria texana	Texas seymeria
Stemodia schottii	Schott's stemodia
Verbascum thapsus	common mullein
Veronica peregrina	wandering veronica

Sellaginaceae · Sellaginaceae

Selaginella lepidophylla	resurrection plant
Selaginella underwoodii	Underwood's spikemoss
Selaginella wrightii	Wright's spikemoss

Simaroubaceae · Simaroubaceae

Castela erecta ssp. texana — goatbush

Smilacaceae · Smilacaceae

Smilax bona-nox — common greenbriar

Solanaceae · Solanaceae

Calibrachoa parviflora	mudflat petunia
Chamaesaracha coniodes	gray five eyes
Chamaesaracha pallida	pale false nightshade
Chamaesaracha sordida	hairy false nightshade
Chamaesaracha villosa	Trans-Pecos five-eyes
Datura inoxia	Indian apple
Datura wrightii	Wright's jimsonweed
Hunzikeria texana	Texas cupflower
Lycium berlandieri	Berlandier wolfberry
Nicotiana glauca	tree tobacco
Nicotiana repanda	fiddleleaf tobacco
Nicotiana trigonophylla	desert tobacco
Physalis cinerascens var. cinerascens	beach groundcherry
Quincula lobata	purple groundcherry
Solanum elaeagnifolium	silverleaf nightshade
Solanum ptychanthum	American nightshade
Solanum rostratum	buffalobur
Solanum triquetrum	Texas nightshade

Sterculiaceae · Sterculiaceae

Ayenia pilosa	dwarf ayenia
Hermannia texana	Texas hermannia
Melochia pyramidata	angelpod melochia

Tamaricaceae · Tamaricaceae

Tamarix aphylla	athel
Tamarix ramosissima	salt cedar

Thelypteridaceae · Thelypteridaceae

Thelypteris ovata var. lindheimeri — Lindheimer's Maiden Fern

Typhaceae · Typhaceae

Typha domingensis — tule

Ulmaceae

Scientific name	Common name
Celtis laevigata var. laevigata	sugar hackberry
Celtis laevigata var. reticulata	netleaf hackberry
Celtis pallida	granjeno
Ulmus pumila	Chinese elm

Urticaceae

Scientific name	Common name
Boehmeria cylindrica	false nettle
Parietaria pensylvanica	Pennsylvania pellitory
Urtica chamaedryoides	stinging nettle

Verbenaceae

Aloysia gratissima	beebrush
Bouchea linifolia	groovestem bouchea
Glandularia bipinnatifida	Dakota mock vervain
Glandularia bipinnatifida var. bipinnatifida	Dakota vervain
Glandularia pumila	low pink vervain
Glandularia quandrangulata	beaked vervain
Glandularia tumidula	Plains vervain
Lantana achyranthifolia	brushland lantana
Lantana urticoides	calico bush
Lantana velutina	velvet lantana
Lippia graveolens	scented lippia
Phyla nodiflora	frogfruit
Tetraclea coulteri	Coulter's wrinklefruit
Verbena bipinnatifida	Dakota mock vervain
Verbena canescens	gray vervain
Verbena halei	slender vervain
Verbena neomexicana	New Mexico vervain
Verbena perennis	perennial vervain
Verbena plicata	whitevein vervain
Verbena scabra	sandpaper vervain
Vitex agnus-castus	chastetree

Violaceae

Scientific name	Common name
Hybanthus verticillatus	green violet

Viscaceae

Scientific name	Common name
Phoradendron tomentosum	mistletoe

Vitaceae

Cissus trifoliata	cow itch, ivy treebine
Parthenocissus heptaphylla	sevenleaf creeper
Parthenocissus quinquefolia	Virginia creeper
Vitis cinerea var. helleri	Heller's grape
Vitis monticola	mountain grape
Vitis rupestris	sand grape

Zannichelliaceae

Scientific name	Common name
Zannichellia palustris	common poolmat

Zygophyllaceae

Guaiacum angustifolium	guayacan
Kallstroemia hirsutissima	carpetweed
Kallstroemia parviflora	warty caltrop
Larrea tridentata	creosotebush

NPS 621/106585, February 2011